DAVID **GROVER** / SEVEN **VINTON**

DIGITAL TECHNOLOGIES FOR THE AUSTRALIAN CURRICULUM
A PROJECT–BASED APPROACH
YEARS 9 AND 10

Digital Technologies for the Australian Curriculum: A Project-based Approach

Years 9 & 10

1st Edition

David Grover

Seven Vinton

Contributors: Heather Knights and Eamon Gormley

Publishing editor: Lizzie Allmand

Project editor: Kathryn Coulehan

Proofreader: Bree DeRoche

Cover design: Aisling Gallagher

Text design: Aisling Gallagher

Cover image: iStock.com/Veronaa

Permissions researcher: Helen Mammides

Production controller: Christine Fotis

Typeset by: MPS Limited

Any URLs contained in this publication were checked for currency during the production process. Note, however, that the publisher cannot vouch for the ongoing currency of URLs.

For product information and technology assistance,

in Australia call **1300 790 853**;

in New Zealand call **0800 449 725**

For permission to use material from this text or product, please email **aust.permissions@cengage.com**

Cengage Learning Australia

Level 7, 80 Dorcas Street

South Melbourne, Victoria Australia 3205

Cengage Learning New Zealand

Unit 4B Rosedale Office Park

331 Rosedale Road, Albany, North Shore 0632, NZ

For learning solutions, visit **cengage.com.au**

Printed in Malaysia by Papercraft.

8 9 10 11 25 24

National Library of Australia Cataloguing-in-Publication Data

Grover, David, author.

Digital technologies for the Australian curriculum : a project-based approach years 9 and 10 / David Grover, Seven Vinton.

9780170411820 (paperback)

Secondary school age.

Information technology--Curriculum planning.

Computer programming--Study and teaching (Secondary)

Information technology--Australia--Textbooks.

Computer software--Problems, exercises, etc.

Software maintenance--Textbooks.

Vinton, Seven, author.

CONTENTS

INTRODUCTION

Digital Technologies for the Australian Curriculum: A Project-based Approach is a project-based creative resource for students and teachers, comprehensively covering all Stage 4 and 5 outcomes for the Australian Curriculum: Digital Technologies.

The two workbooks, one for each stage, together with accompanying online resources, establish students' knowledge in the core Knowledge and Understanding topics, then build understanding using a variety of learning approaches such as guided projects, knowledge probes, skill builders, activities, class group work, web probes and research tasks.

After acquiring a topic's necessary foundational skills, students build practical skills by developing their own digital solutions through a selection of practical projects.

Reflecting the pattern established in the curriculum, all projects follow the progression: Defining, Designing, Implementing and Evaluating.

Teachers can select from more than 40 individual and group-based projects in five topic areas serving a wide range of ability levels. The projects emphasise creativity and challenge while building on essential knowledge and skills. Many include further extensions or advanced options. Online teacher resources offer a variety of options for flexible implementation in the school.

Key ideas specified in the digital technologies curriculum of project management, systems thinking, design thinking, computational thinking and creating preferred futures are addressed.

The workbooks and associated online resources embrace the curriculum's core competencies of literacy, numeracy, ICT, critical and creative thinking, personal and social capability, ethical understanding and intercultural understanding.

HOW TO USE THIS BOOK

Digital Technologies for the Australian Curriculum: A Project-based Approach Years 9 and 10 is divided into two parts. Part One: Knowledge and Understanding covers the **core** units outlined by the curriculum and Part Two: Projects provides opportunities for students to explore the concepts and skills discussed earlier and to test their knowledge of digital technology through the application of IT skills. The book has the following features:

- **ACARA outcomes** are listed on chapter opening pages where applicable.
- **Glossary terms** are listed on chapter opening pages where applicable and highlighted in text.
- **Infobits** provide snippets of useful and interesting information to stimulate curiosity.
- **Web probes** encourage students to go online and complete further investigations.

- **Activities** contain a variety of practical tasks that can be completed as a class in groups, individually or as homework.
- **Knowledge probes** highlight activities that require greater depth of discovery and higher-order thinking.
- **Skill builders** are tasks that will develop a particular skill.
- **Data files** such as Excel spreadsheets, coding files and images required by students to complete certain projects or activities can be found on the *Digital Technologies 9 & 10* website: https://www.nelsonnet.com.au/free-resources/nelson-technology/digital-technologies-9-10-workbook-1ed.
- **Weblinks** to useful websites are supplied on the *Digital Technologies 9 & 10* website.
- **Screenshots** are included throughout to provide students with clear visual cues to follow.

9780170411820

ABOUT THE AUTHORS

David Grover has been Head Teacher of Computing at Chatswood High School, New South Wales and is the author of a number of texts and online resources for the Australian Curriculum in Digital Technologies and for senior secondary computing. He conducts workshops in computing technology for teachers at a number of tertiary institutions and has served as a senior examination marker.

David has conducted research in educational applications of augmented reality (AR) and in digital creativity for learning for Macquarie University and at present is enjoying combining AR with 3D printing! He loves sharing his excitement for emerging technologies with students and many have gone on to enjoy successful careers in animation, games design, robotics and programming. He has established a reputation for his expertise in interactive digital education, recognised in various teaching awards and a NSW Premier's Scholarship where he studied New and Emerging Technologies in educational institutions around the globe.

Seven Vinton is the co-inventor of the ARD2-INNOV8 Shield for Arduino. Prior to his 18 years of teaching, Seven worked in the areas of industrial arts and technologies, running a small business in ceramic parts and mold-making. He has enjoyed a life-long passion for digital technologies, and has completed programming courses in C++, Python, MATLAB, IoT and Digital Interfacing.

Seven currently holds the position of Curriculum Leader at Oberon High School in Geelong and also teaches classes in VCE Studio Arts, Engineering, and Digital Technologies. He has held several other leadership positions in his teaching career, including VCAL Coordinator, Professional Learning Leader, and eLearning Leader. Seven has run and participated in many regional and state-level presentations that have been aimed at building capacity of digital learning for both students and teachers.

Seven has dedicated much of his time over the past four years towards finding and promoting solutions that help support students with programming digital devices.

UNDERSTANDING DATA COMPRESSION

OUTCOMES

Australian curriculum content descriptions:
- Investigate how digital systems represent text, image and audio data in binary (ACTDIK024) (AC)
- Analyse simple compression of data and how content data are separated from presentation (ACTDIK035) (AC)

GLOSSARY

codec Software that both codes and decodes digital data (from the two words coder-decoder), often to achieve compression of a file or data stream intended for transmission or storage

compression Process of representing digital information using fewer bits in order to reduce file size by simplifying data or by removing non-critical data

lossless compression Algorithm that reduces file size by representing the data more efficiently. One lossless method replaces repeated bit patterns with shorter tokens. This method of compression is important when it is critical for decompressed data to be an exact copy of the original; for example, in text documents, programming source code or archiving. No data is lost and the original file can be perfectly reconstructed

lossy compression Algorithm that reduces file size by permanently discarding redundant or unnecessary information not critical for users. The reconstructed file is an approximation of the original; for example, in audio compression by eliminating frequencies outside the range of human hearing or in image compression by combining or averaging pixels

run length encoding (RLE) A lossless compression technique where recurring patterns in binary sequences are replaced with shorter patterns recorded in a table

THE NEED FOR COMPRESSION

We learnt in *Digital Technologies 7 & 8* (Chapter 2) that binary digits (bits) in a raster graphics file represent the colour of each pixel. In an audio file they may represent the pitch of a note. The more accurate we want the colour or the sound to be, the longer these strings of bits will be. Imagine how many are required to represent a full-length movie, where many separate images must be stored then displayed at up to 60 frames a second!

A three-minute song can be 30 MB and a one-hour movie can be as much as 800 GB. This would just use too much space. We need a way to compress data before we store it or transmit it. In this chapter you will learn how sounds and images can be reduced to one third of their size and still sound and look good.

Activity: Compression everywhere!

1 We use **compression** techniques when we use abbreviations in text messaging. What messages do these represent when texting?

BFF _____

IMHO _____

B4N _____

OIC _____

Is any meaning lost using acronyms such as these?

2 Keyboard-based emoticons are a form of text compression. What is meant by each of the following emoticons?

:-D _____

:'(_____

:$ _____

Is meaning lost using emoticons such as these?

3 Emoji are a pictorial compression tool. Research the origins of emoji and where the word comes from. How would you interpret the following emoji (see Figure 1.1)?

From shutterstock.com. Top: Yayayoyo; ober-art; Petrovic Igor. Bottom: all Yayayoyo.

Figure 1.1

_____

_____

IMAGE COMPRESSION

You already know two ways to reduce the file size of an image:

- reduce the number of pixels in the image
- reduce the bit depth for each pixel. (You learnt about bit depth or colour depth in *Digital Technologies 7 & 8*.)

We will examine what happens to a painting when it goes through various digital changes.

First it is digitised using a camera. It loses original colour data in this process. Even so, the file can be over 200 MB. When the painting in Figure 1.2 was first digitised (by photographing it using a high-quality digital camera) the original paint colours are approximated by the digital camera using a more limited palette.

Shutterstock.com/Fresh Stock

Figure 1.2

Next we can reduce the bit depth of the image to 3 bits (the number of bits representing each pixel) so the different number of binary codes available is now only $2^3 = 8$ colours (see Figure 1.3). The file size is now 3 MB.

Compression techniques can be either lossy or lossless.

Figure 1.3 Here the original digital image has had its colour palette reduced to just eight colours. Can you identify them? The file size is now around 3 MB.

Lossy image compression

One method of **lossy compression** relies on reducing the colour palette – the number of colours for a particular image.

There are many ways this can be done, but JPEG (named after the Joint Photographic Experts Group) does this by relying on the characteristics of the human eye.

The JPEG algorithm analyses and ranks pixel data on its importance to human visual perception and throws away the less important information. The resolution of the image is reduced but we do not notice it.

Humans don't see small changes in brightness or colour very well. Many optical illusions depend on this. We interpret the brightness and colour of pixels by contrast with ones that are adjacent. The eye is most sensitive when these variations occur across just a few pixels, otherwise we do not see them. If pixel brightness data is separated from hue (actual colour), data the human eye does not notice can be averaged when these differences are small.

Users can select the amount of compression and when an image has a lot of gradient colour this approach can reduce file sizes by up to 10 times! This compression method always results in some loss of quality, since colour information is removed.

In Figure 1.4 JPEG compression has reduced the original 200 MB file to less than 1 MB.

Highest quality

Medium quality

Lowest quality

Figure 1.4 JPEG compression is a lossy format. Nearly every digital camera can save images in the JPEG format. JPEG files degrade when repeatedly edited and saved. The JPEG format is also used by the image compression algorithm in Adobe PDF documents.

Figure 1.5 JPEG compression results in further loss of colour data but the original 200 MB file size is now reduced to 200 KB! These changes are not obvious to the human eye (compare to Figure 1.2) but are seen when enlarging the detail in a red petal. The image in the middle has been enlarged from Figure 1.2. The image on the right has been enlarged from the compressed image on the left.

Activity: Experiments reducing image sizes

Use a high-resolution image (example search term: 'Van Gogh Starry Night Google Art Project.jpg') and record the following approaches to reducing file size. Save each file and record its size each time from your computer's file directory. Remember to start with the original file for each method!

Extension: Open your original image and choose Image > Mode > Indexed colour... with eight colours. Next select from the Photoshop menu Image > Colour table... and select individual colours to change them.

Table 1.1

Method of file size reduction using Photoshop	File size in MB	Image quality (1 low–5 high)	% reduction in file size	File size
Your original image				
Reduce image dimensions Image > Image size... (make sure resampling option is checked)				
Reduce colour depth Image > Mode > Indexed colour				
Save as highest quality JPG File > Save As... then select quality setting				
Save as lowest quality JPG File > Save As... then select quality setting				
(Select and describe another method)				

Lossless image compression

With **lossless compression** the decompressed file is restored exactly with no loss of data. A compression approach called **run length encoding (RLE)** achieves this lossless compression in image files.

RLE compression happens at the level of the binary code itself by looking for recurring patterns in the sequences of 1s (ones) and 0s (zeros), and replacing these with shorter codes and recording the changes in a table.

GIF and PNG formats both use this approach and so are lossless methods. The original image can be repeatedly saved and opened again with no loss of data. Figure 1.6 illustrates this method.

Each number represents the colour of a pixel on the screen.

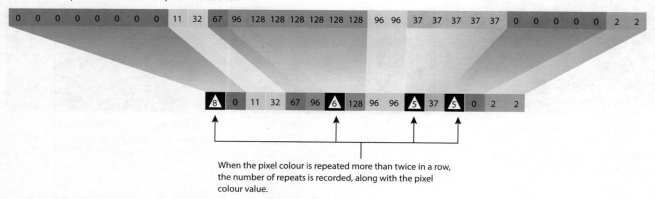

When the pixel colour is repeated more than twice in a row, the number of repeats is recorded, along with the pixel colour value.

Figure 1.6 Lossless compression in a GIF image file explained

9780170411820

There are quite complicated algorithms built on this principle, which you may study if you do further computing science. One is the LZW (Lempel-Ziv-Welch) method. The GIF image format uses this method of lossless compression.

QãMRPQhÉË/Ò
Éƒ]√ÄÄÄÄÄÄÄÄÄÄÄUãÏãuÔ"VãÒ«t.ã¬Wçxç§$ãÉ¿Ñ…u˜+«PRãŒÉúÔ   ãÒ¿_t
âHã∆^]¬ÄÄÄÄÄÄÄÄUãÏjçEPãŒ«ÉjÒ   ãÒ¿t«@ã∆]¬ÄÄÄÄÄÄÄUãÏãuÔ"ã¡âtÉ
√3¿√ÄÄÄãÒ¿tãHçDv∏˙˙Yv√ÄÄÄÄÄÄÄÄÄÄÄãÒ¿tã@É¿Ò¿u
˜Y…ã¡Î∏LcbÒ…tQPÉñ=ÉƒÒ¿u∞√2¿√ÄÄÄÄÄÄÄÄÄÄPÈ˙Ò
Ò¿Î¿√ÄÄÄãÒ¿tã@É¿√∏Lcb√ÄÄÄÄÄÄÄÄÄÄÄÄà√ÄÄÄÄÄÄÄÄÄÄÄÄUãÏ3…âHàHâ
âHâHãMâàP]√ÄÄUãÏj˜h<¿Xd°PQSVW° 1]3≈PçEÙd£ÉŒˇˆ®Õbu(É
®ÕbhÕb«E¸Ëâh¿WYÉóÈÈƒãu¸°$ÕbÕ¿t

Figure 1.8 A text editor will attempt to represent strings of 0s and 1s as their ASCII characters when opening non-text files.

1   Open any jpg file using your text editor (such as Windows' Notepad or Apple's TextEdit) and delete a small section of the file – towards the end of the file. Rename the file as, say, *test.jpg* and resave it. Open it in an image application. What do you notice?

_____

_____

_____

_____

2   Look for a frequently occurring character string in the test.jpg text file and use the Find and Replace function in your text editor to replace that string with something else of the same length. Open it in an image application. What do you notice?

_____

_____

_____

_____

INFOBIT

Which image format should you choose? JPEG, TIFF, GIF, PSD, BMP, PICT, or PNG? Here are some general guidelines:
- If the image is to be used on a website or a mobile device, use JPEG, PNG or GIF.
- If you wish to retain a transparent background, use PNG or PSD (Photoshop).
- If the image is to appear in high-quality print, use TIFF.
- When working with images, always save an original version of your image in your software's native file format such as PSD format for Photoshop.

Knowledge probe: Opening files using a text editor

If you were to look at any digital file, no matter whether its destination was a word processor, image-editing software such as Photoshop, database, web browser or other software application, all you would see would be 1s and 0s.

Knowledge Probe

Figure 1.7 All digital files are strings of 0s (zeros) and 1s (ones).

It is up to the software application and the hardware to interpret these 0s and 1s correctly – perhaps as characters in an alphabet, colours in a bit mapped image, a data item in a database or other data types as explained in Chapter 2 of *Digital Technologies 7 & 8*.

Most computers have a text editor application included (such as Windows' Notepad or Apple's TextEdit). However, these are designed only to interpret files as text files. If you try to open other file types with them you will usually see strange characters as shown in Figure 1.8. Your text editor will attempt to represent all zeros and ones as ASCII characters, as it cannot know what the binary codes really represent.

TEXT COMPRESSION

In the case of text compression, it is vital that compression is lossless, for obvious reasons. This is particularly critical when compressing programming code files. When decompressed it must be an exact copy!

Text compression uses methods similar to lossless image compression to achieve this. Repeated longer patterns are replaced by shorter code segments recorded in a table. This table is sent along with the compressed file and an exact copy of the original version can be reclaimed.

Lossless compression widget: Code.org has a great widget you can use to perform lossless compression on text interactively. Try it out!

The zip file compression method uses a version of this method.

iStock.com/matejmo

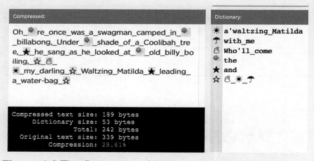
VIDEO COMPRESSION

Compression for video uses algorithms known as **codecs** (compressors-decompressors). There are many types. Some are designed to reduce file size and others are designed to speed up file transfer over the Internet.

These codecs have names like Cinepak, MPEG-4 and Sorenson. Such products as Apple's QuickTime and Windows Media Player have built-in codecs. These can be lossless (producing usually high-quality large files) or lossy (low quality, small files).

Video compression uses similar methods as image file compression, but a big problem is that a video must play smoothly at many frames per second. Such rapid decompression would take far too long and require too much computing power using just these methods. For video, additional compression tricks have been invented.

Because adjacent frames of a video are usually only slightly different from each other, a common method records only the data in the image that change between frames. For example, a movie of a person passing the camera only needs the person to be redrawn and part of the background the person has just left (see Figure 1.10).

MPEG compression for video uses this approach and can reduce video file sizes by up to 200:1. This method is also used in audio compression, where only the differences between successive sound samples are recorded.

Key frame
The opening image of a compressed video sequence contains all the data relating to the image.

Selected data
Subsequent frames contain only data that relates to the actor's new position and the area he previously occupied.

The result
Subsequent frames can be drawn using a fraction of the data contained in the key frame.

Figure 1.10 By only transmitting the data that changes in a movie frame, a lot of compression is possible.

A further approach is to record video data at fewer frames per second so that file sizes are reduced, making lower demands on the processor. The trade-off will be a lower-quality image that may appear 'jumpy'. The lowest possible frame rate for acceptable animation is 8 fps. Realistic motion requires higher frame rates and motion pictures use 60 fps. It is sometimes possible to see flickering or strange artifacts when decompression fails to keep up in a streaming video.

AUDIO COMPRESSION

In *Digital Technology 7 & 8* Chapter 2, we studied audio sample rates, sample sizes and stereo. For audio files, simple compression can be achieved by:

- reducing the sample rate (the number of sound samples taken per second)
- making audio mono rather than stereo (this will halve the size)
- reducing the sample size (the number of bits used to code the sound sample)

Figure 1.11 illustrates these techniques. All of these are lossy techniques.

However, as in the case of video data, we can use techniques that rely on the talent our brains have of being able to fill in missing data and completely reconstruct the meaning of an original message. The MP3 audio format achieves even further compression by eliminating frequencies the human ear cannot detect. This involves loss of data, although you would not be likely to notice the reduced quality. Great gains in file size reduction can be achieved using this lossy technique.

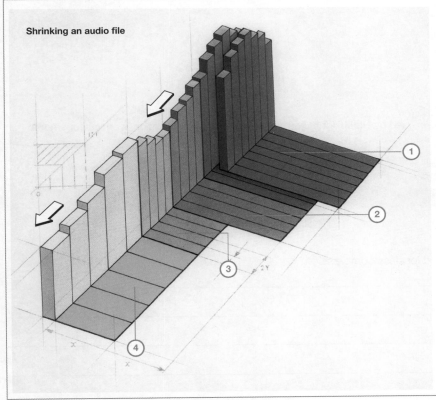

Shrinking an audio file

Dorling Kindersley

Sound files can be made smaller by a factor of 16 or more, but unfortunately the quality drops too.

1 **The original sound file** The original audio file was sampled at 44 000 samples per second. Here each sample is represented by one blue vertical bar using 16 binary digits, or bits to measure each sample.

2 **Stereo to mono** The simplest way to shrink a file is to combine the two stereo channels, left and right into one mono channel.

3 **Halve the bits** By using 8 bits instead of 16 to measure each sample, the file is smaller but the sound will be less precise and 'grittier'.

4 **Halve the samples** To shrink the file still further we can reduce the number of samples taken per second, making the sound 'muddier'.

Figure 1.11 How sound files can be compressed

Activity: Scrambled!

We have discovered that lossy compression in both audio and visual data depends on the way the human brain handles data by interpreting what is missing. This is also the way we interpret animation and movies as continuous movement.

You may be familiar with the following well-known example showing how our brains can interpret this scrambled message to regain its meaning. The first and last letters of each word are in their correct places and others are scrambled. Try to read this aloud:

Aoccdrnig to rsceearhers, it deosn't mttaer in waht oredr the ltteers in a wrod are, the olny iprmoetnt tihng is taht the frist and lsat ltteer be at the rghit pclae. The rset can be a toatl mses and you can sitll raed it wouthit a porbelm. Tihs is bcuseae the huamn mnid deos not raed ervey lteter by istlef, but the wrod as a wlohe.

1 Follow the weblink from the *Digital Technologies 9 & 10* website or find similar site that generates scrambled sentences and test how well our brains fill in the missing data by requiring a partner to read the scrambled versions, and then swap roles.

2 **Advanced programming challenge:** Try to code a computer program that does this!

Weblink

1   Determine which type of data each of these file formats handles and identify each as either lossy or lossless, or both.

Table 1.2

File type	Full name	Data type(s)	Lossy or lossless compression?
JPEG			
TIFF			
MP3			
GIF			
TXT			
ZIP			
PNG			
BMP			
MPEG			

2   **Taking it further:** Find out what technique is used by Netflix for movie streaming where compression is critical for smooth viewing.

REVIEW

Identify

1   What is the difference between lossy and lossless compression?

_____

_____

_____

_____

2   Give two examples each of lossy and lossless compression.

_____

_____

_____

_____

3   Why is compression used in digital technologies?

_____

_____

_____

_____

9780170411820

Analyse

4 Explain how JPEG compression reduces the size of graphics files.

_____

_____

_____

_____

5 Explain how RLE compression works and identify it as lossy or lossless.

_____

_____

_____

_____

_____

6 Give examples where each of the following graphics formats would be most suitable: JPEG, TIFF, GIF, PNG.

_____

_____

_____

_____

_____

7 Outline one method of audio compression.

_____

_____

_____

_____

_____

Research

8 Find out the difference between a codec and tools such as QuickTime or AVFoundation (Mac and iOS) and Video for Windows or DirectShow (Windows).

_____

_____

_____

_____

_____

02 UNDERSTANDING ENCRYPTION

OUTCOMES

Australian curriculum content descriptions:
- Investigate how data is transmitted and secured in wired, wireless and mobile networks, and how the specifications affect performance (ACTDIK023) *AC*
- Acquire data from a range of sources and evaluate authenticity, accuracy and timeliness (ACTDIP025) *AC*
- Develop techniques for acquiring, storing and validating quantitative and qualitative data from a range of sources, considering privacy and security requirements (ACTDIP036) *AC*

GLOSSARY

asymmetric cryptography A method of encryption in which two different keys are required consisting of a *public key* and a *private key*. The public key is used to encrypt data that can be decrypted *only* using the private key. Also known as public-key encryption

encryption The process of encoding data so that it is incomprehensible to others and can be decoded only by the intended receiver

hash function A method used to map longer strings of binary data to shorter strings of fixed lengths. Also known as hashing algorithm

secret key A piece of information that is kept hidden from unintended recipients and needed by the recipient to decrypt an encoded message

symmetric encryption A method of encryption in which the same key is used for both encryption and decryption

9780170411820

WHAT IS CRYPTOGRAPHY?

Ever since humans existed they seem to have wanted to keep secrets. The need to keep secrets has driven the invention of thousands of techniques for making codes, but encoding is not just for secrets. Human languages, Aboriginal rock art, texting abbreviations and even the way we dress and smile are all forms of encoding messages. Early Christians used a fish symbol to mark their meeting places and children often use secret invented languages to conceal things from adults (and adults often do the same in reverse!).

Figure 2.1 Secret codes have been used for thousands of years. Find out why Indigenous Australians used codes and why Leonardo da Vinci wrote in his notebooks using mirror writing.

INFOBIT: AN UNSOLVED PROBLEM IN MATHEMATICS

No one has yet been able to prove that a true one-way function exists. It is one of the great unsolved problems of mathematics and cryptography.

Coding is a valuable skill to possess, but an even more valuable one is to be able to access and control the coded information. The central goal of cryptography is to create a true one-way function. That is, one that is easy to calculate for any input, but very hard to reverse, even when the code-breaker possesses lots of examples.

War and espionage have often been the reason for the invention of secret codes and these began to be widely used in Europe in the 16th century. Human beings have developed ingenious ways to disguise messages and each new coding method becomes a challenge for cryptoanalysts. The breaking of the Enigma code used by Germany in the Second World War remains the most famous example of code breaking.

Today computerised communication affects all areas of our lives and **encryption** and privacy now concern everyone who uses a computer or mobile device.

Every encryption method is ultimately cracked and so must continually be replaced or updated. This unit will help you understand how encryption works.

Figure 2.2 A captured German Enigma machine and Colossus, the first programmed computer, used by Alan Turing's team to crack the Enigma code.

Symmetric versus asymmetric encryption

The most famous people in cryptography are three fictional characters, Alice (A) and Bob (B) who wish to send messages to one another, and Eve ('Eavesdropper'). These three have traditionally been used to explain encryption methods.

Symmetric encryption

Alice wishes to send a secret message to Bob. In symmetric secret-key encryption, such as a Caesar shift, Alice and Bob use a single **secret key**, held by them both, to encrypt and decrypt data (see Figure 2.4).

In the symmetric Caesar shift code, Alice needs to send Bob the key (e.g. 'shift letters three places'). If Eve intercepts both the message and the key, then the message can be easily cracked.

Both Alice and Bob must protect this key because if Eve has the key, she could use it to decrypt the message and read it or even change the message, encrypt it and claim it originated from either Alice or Bob.

Secret-key encryption is classified as **symmetric encryption** because the same key is used for encryption and decryption. Secret-key encryption algorithms are very fast but are easy to crack if the key is intercepted.

Video:
Cybersecurity jobs

Figure 2.3 Fictional characters used to explain cryptography: Alice, Bob and Eve

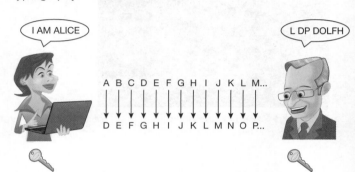

Figure 2.4 In a Caesar shift, each letter in a message is shifted a set number of places in the alphabet (here three spaces). Alice and Bob use a single secret key, held by them both, to encrypt and decrypt data. Anyone with the key can decrypt the message.

Skill builder: Programming and cracking a symmetric Caesar shift code

The Roman general Julius Caesar (100–44 BCE) often wrote in his correspondence about secret writing and even used it in letters to friends. His most famous method used a simple shift of the alphabet.

Skill builder

For example, if the letter A is to be encrypted, and the shift is three letters, then A appears encrypted as D, B as E, C as F and so on.

This means there are only 25 possible ciphers and 25 possible 'keys' (to unlock the code).

In this activity we will automate Caesar shift encryption by building a spreadsheet. Then we will try to crack the

message using the most well-known method of looking at letter frequencies. Each human language uses some letters more often than others. In English the most common letter is 'e' followed by 't' and 'a'.

How would this method of using frequencies work?

_____

_____

_____

_____

Table 2.1 Caesar shift of three spaces

Plain alphabet	Cipher alphabet	Plain alphabet	Cipher alphabet	Plain alphabet	Cipher alphabet	Plain alphabet	Cipher alphabet
A	D	H	K	O	R	V	Y
B	E	I	L	P	S	W	Z
C	F	J	M	Q	T	X	A
D	G	K	N	R	U	Y	B
E	H	L	O	S	V	Z	C
F	I	M	P	T	W		
G	J	N	Q	U	X		

Spreadsheet functions you will need

(Refer also to the ASCII table in *Digital Technologies 7 & 8*, page 25.)

Table 2.2

Excel formula	What the formula does
=CODE()	Returns the ASCII value of the character supplied. For example, =CODE("A") returns 65.
=CHAR()	Returns the character matching a decimal ASCII value supplied. For example, =CHAR(65) returns the character 'A'.
=IF(logical_test, [value_if_true], [value_if_false])	For example, =IF(A1>50, "big", "small") will return the word 'big' if the value in A1 is greater than 50, and return 'small' otherwise.
=MOD(number, divisor)	Returns the remainder after number is divided by divisor. For example, =MOD(12,5) will return the value 2.

Note: CODE is the inverse of CHAR.

So the formula =CODE(CHAR(65)) will return 65, because =CHAR(65) returns the character 'A' and =CODE("A") returns 65.

Starting with a three position shift

1 Open a new spreadsheet.

2 Invent a plaintext (message to be encoded) using uppercase, and enter just one letter in each cell down column A. It is important to only use capital letters.

We need to convert each letter to its ASCII decimal value so we can shift it along three letters in the alphabet and then convert it back to a character again.

3 In Column B enter the formula: =CHAR(CODE(A1)+3)

4 Read steps 6 and 7 before proceeding. Now Fill down column B with this formula (if you haven't learnt Fill down, see Chapter 11 in *Digital Technologies 7 & 8*).

5 Explain how this works.

_____

_____

_____

_____

6 Check down column B and notice that the spaces have produced an error.

The following formula fixes this problem:

=IF(A1 <>"", (CHAR(CODE(A1)+3)), "")

Fill down Column C using this improved formula and explain how it works.

_____

_____

_____

_____

7 Observe that the formula will not encrypt some letters properly if they are towards the end of the alphabet. Try entering 'X' or 'Y' or 'Z' in your plaintext message in a cell of column A and see what happens. Explain why.

_____

_____

_____

_____

_____

8 The ASCII value for the letter 'A' is 65. The following formula fixes the alphabet wrap problem in '7':

=CHAR(MOD(CODE(A1)+3-65,26)+65)

Fill down column D with this formula and explain how it allows letters to wrap back to the beginning of the alphabet.

_____

_____

_____

_____

_____

9 The following formula combines the last two. Can you see how it does this?

It solves both our problems: spaces and alphabet wrapping.

Fill down column E with this formula.

```
=IF(A1<>"",CHAR(MOD((CODE
(A1)+3-65),26)+65)," ")
```

Explain how this formula works.

_____

_____

_____

_____

10 Challenge: Can you write a formula in column F that decodes column E back to the letters appearing in column A?

_____

_____

_____

_____

_____

Note: A finished version of this activity is in the online resources on the *Digital Technologies 9 & 10* website as an Excel file titled *caesar_code*.

Skill builder: Using letter frequency analysis to crack code

1 Take your encoded message from the last activity and enter it in the frequency analysis widget from Code.org.

2 Use the Shift-right button until you crack the code. Notice how the frequency bars will closely match up when the code is cracked.

Weblink

Skill builder

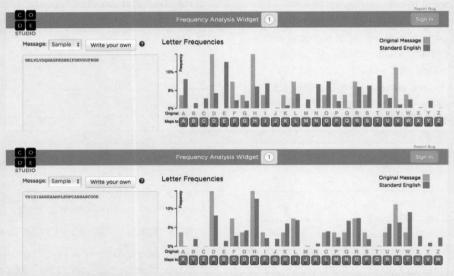

Figure 2.5 (top) Original code and (bottom) the solution using letter frequency analysis

3 Explain how this works.

_____

_____

_____

_____

_____

_____

_____

9780170411820

Asymmetric encryption

Public-key cryptography (also known as RSA after its inventors' initials) is an example of **asymmetric cryptography**. Here two different keys are required.

Suppose Bob wishes to send a secret message to Alice. Using public-key cryptography, Alice generates mathematically linked *key pairs*, consisting of a *public key* and a *private key*. Alice shares her public key with Bob, and anyone else who wants to send her a message, but the private key is known *only* to her. If a public key is used to encrypt data, then it can be decrypted only using her private key. This private key is never shared.

For Alice to send a secret message back to Bob, she must encrypt it using Bob's public key and Bob must use his private key to decrypt it (see Figure 2.6). Even if Eve now

gets a copy of the public key, which is easy because it is sent openly, she still cannot read the message because she does not have a copy of Bob's private key. Of course, it is vital that no one ever shares their private key.

Public-key encryption is classified as asymmetric encryption because different keys are used for encryption and decryption. Asymmetric encryption is a good example of a *one-way function*. Once the message is encrypted, it is virtually impossible to reverse without the private key.

Combining both methods

As public-key algorithms are very slow, they are usually used in combination with secret-key cryptography. This is because public-key encryption takes so much computing power that it is not used for the actual message. Instead it is only used to transfer a secret (symmetric) key so that regular, two-way secret-key encryption can be used for the remainder of the messaging. Of course in today's online world, the symmetric method is not a simple one like the Caesar cipher. When you see 'https://' beginning a web address, it is this combination that is being used to protect your data.

Video: View the excellent videos explaining public-key encryption at Khan Academy

Alice's public key

Alice's public key

Alice's private key

Bob wants to send a secret message to Alice. Alice shares her public key with Bob, who uses it to encrypt his message and then sends it to Alice.

Alice uses her private key to decrypt the message she received from Bob.

Figure 2.6 Using public-key cryptography, Alice generates mathematically linked *key pairs*, consisting of a *public key* and a *private key*.

INFOBIT: HASH FUNCTIONS

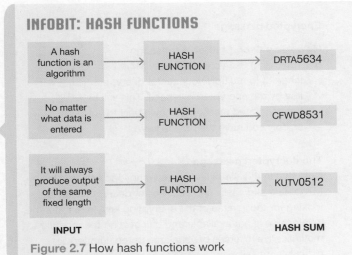

INPUT		HASH SUM
A hash function is an algorithm	HASH FUNCTION	DRTA5634
No matter what data is entered	HASH FUNCTION	CFWD8531
It will always produce output of the same fixed length	HASH FUNCTION	KUTV0512

A **hash function** is an algorithm that produces output of the same length every time when given input data. Also, it is designed to always produce the same output when given identical input. It is used to speed up searches on large amounts of data, as the hash function is used as the index to the data.

In cryptography a hash function could be used by two people to confirm each possesses identical information, but where neither is willing to reveal it first! Imagine both Alice and Bob are spies and claim to know the identity of a traitor among them. Alice and Bob could both calculate the hash for the name of the traitor and check that their two hashes are the same.

Figure 2.7 How hash functions work

In this activity you will simulate the concept behind public–private key encryption. Although the actual method is more complex, the general principles are the same.

1 With your teacher's help, get an understanding of modular arithmetic and practice multiplication using the Code.org widget for modular arithmetic as part of its CSP course. Follow the weblink from the *Digital Technologies 9 & 10* website.

2 Next complete this modular 7 (M7) multiplication table.

Table 2.3

M7	0	1	2	3	4	5	6
0							
1							
2							
3							
4							
5							
6							

Public–private key encryption

Public–private key encryption is based on modular arithmetic and prime numbers. It depends on the idea that no mathematician has ever discovered a pattern or algorithm for predicting prime numbers. If this ever happens, then worldwide Internet security would be destroyed. This has been called a doomsday scenario! Even young children can multiply two primes, but the reverse operation of splitting a large number into two prime factors is much harder and the primes used in encryption are hundreds of digits long.

Let us imagine that you are Alice, and Bob wants to send you an important secret message (perhaps her secret symmetric key) using public–private key encryption. We simulate public-key encryption here using the M7 multiplication table you completed above.

This activity is to help you understand a central principle behind this difficult concept. In this example it would not be hard to crack the message.

Note that our first 'message' must be restricted to an integer between 1 and 8.

Remember you are Alice, and Bob wants to send you his secret message.

How Alice generates her public and private keys

1 Your public key will be shared with Bob. Here it is 7 because you chose the modular 7 multiplication table. Write this number in the adjacent box.

Public key

2 You now pick two integers in the table whose mod product is 1 (e.g. 2 and 4). Your encryption key is the first integer and is also shared as part of your public key.

Encryption key

3 Your decryption key, or private key, is the second integer and is kept secret by you.

Decryption key

So, in summary: Alice gives others two numbers: her public and encryption keys but she keeps her private decryption private!

How Bob encrypts his message to Alice

4 Bob chooses a 'message' for secret transmission to Alice (here it needs to be restricted to an integer between 1 and 6). Represent this message using an integer and write it here.

Message (in the form of an integer)

5 Bob knows that public key 7 means he must use the M7 table (shared) to find the product of his message integer and Alice's public encryption key. This result is the encoded secret message he sends to you (Alice). Of course, anyone else can also do this easily.

Encrypted message

How Alice decrypts Bob's message

6 You (Alice) use your public key M7 table (shared) to multiply your secret decryption key by the encrypted message. This will be the decrypted message, known only to you, as only you have the private key.

The decrypted message

Note that in this simplified example anyone who has the M7 table could easily find your secret decryption key by looking for the inverse of the encryption key. In real life, the whole table is not available and discovering the modular multiplicative inverses of very large prime numbers is virtually impossible.

Code.org has an excellent widget that automates public/private key encryption and shows the roles of Alice, Bob and Eve as part of its CSP course.

Weblink

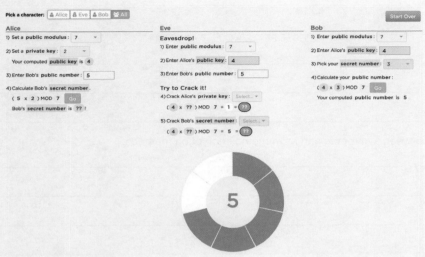

Figure 2.8 The Code.org public–private widget, showing Bob sending Alice a secret message using her public key, which she then decodes using her private key.

REVIEW

Identify

1 Give five early examples of cryptography.

2 Define encryption.

3 What is the purpose of digital encryption?

4 What is a hash function and how is it used?

Analyse

5 Outline how letter frequency analysis works and identify one of its limitations.

_____

_____

_____

_____

_____

6 Explain the difference between symmetric and asymmetric encryption methods.

_____

_____

_____

_____

7 Outline the process by which both Alice and Bob could communicate separate messages to each other using their public and private keys.

_____

_____

_____

_____

_____

_____

_____

Research

8 Research how the German Enigma code worked and summarise how cracking the code affected the outcome of the Second World War.

_____

_____

_____

_____

_____

_____

_____

_____

_____

_____

_____

9780170411820

UNDERSTANDING HOW COMPUTERS WORK

03

OUTCOMES

Australian curriculum content descriptions:
- Investigate the role of hardware and software in managing, controlling and securing the movement of and access to data in networked digital systems (ACTDIK034) *AC*

The **central processing unit (CPU)** is like the heart of your computer. The **fetch-execute cycle** (also machine cycle or instruction cycle) is the main process performed by the CPU in your computer when it runs a program. It is like the engine running your computer. Understanding how it works is the only way to really understand how a computer works and this is your task in this unit.

Figure 3.1 An Intel i7 CPU chip

THE BIG PICTURE

Hardware, software and operating systems

The three categories of software – application, utility and operating system – can be imagined as stacked on top of one another, with each communicating only with those above and below (see Figure 3.2). A computer's operating system interacts with application software and computer hardware.

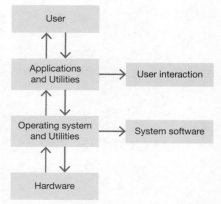

Figure 3.2 The three types of software – application, utility and operating system – communicate only with those immediately above and below. Application software communicates with the operating system and the operating system communicates directly with hardware.

Although the operating system is the first software we see after starting a computer, our regular interaction is mostly with application software through a Graphical User Interface (GUI) provided by the operating system. These usually feature windows, icons, menus and pointer (WIMP). An example is shown in Figure 3.3. Early computers used Command Line Interfaces (CLI) and these are still used by network administrators to control servers. One is shown in Figure 3.4.

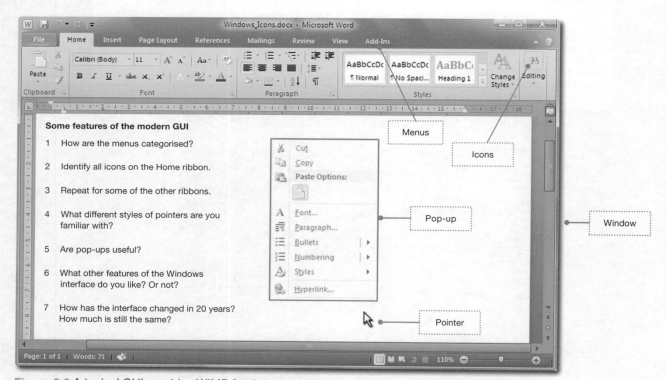

Figure 3.3 A typical GUI provides WIMP for the user and computer to interact. Try the questions listed in the displayed document.

9780170411820

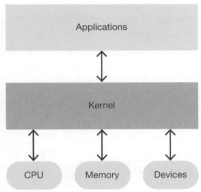

```
Command Prompt
C:\Documents and Settings>dir
Volume in drive C is WINDOWS
Volume Serial Number is 3026-F8D1

Directory of C:\Documents and Settings

08/10/2010  01:25 PM    <DIR>          .
08/10/2010  01:25 PM    <DIR>          ..
08/10/2010  01:25 PM    <DIR>          All Users
08/10/2010  01:45 PM    <DIR>          Jeremy
08/12/2010  08:45 PM    <DIR>          Emma
               0 File(s)              0 bytes
               5 Dir(s)  22,020,505,600 bytes free

C:\Documents and Settings>mem

   655360 bytes total conventional memory
   655360 bytes available to MS-DOS
   599136 largest executable program size

  1048576 bytes total contiguous extended memory
        0 bytes available contiguous extended memory
   941056 bytes available XMS memory
          MS-DOS resident in High Memory Area

C:\DOCUME~1>
```

Figure 3.4 A command line interface. The 'dir' and 'mem' commands are used to display details of the directories and memory usage respectively.

How an operating system works

The operating system (OS) is stored on the hard disk and loaded into RAM as you turn on your computer.

The *kernel* is the main part of your computer's operating system. It manages input and output requests from software and translates these into instructions for the CPU. It also manages peripheral devices such as displays, keyboards, printers, microphones, cameras and speakers. It has the important function of performing *interrupts*, where code the processor is executing is suspended for a more urgent need because you pressed a key or moved your mouse, for example.

An operating system performs six critical tasks:

- **User interface (UI):** it provides a user interface so you can interact with your computer.
- **Application interface:** it provides a way to interact with applications.
- **Security management:** it manages login and permissions.

Figure 3.5 The kernel is the main part of your computer's operating system.

- **Device management:** it manages communication with attached devices.
- **Storage management:** it handles file management and memory.
- **Processor management:** it makes sure that the CPU is working efficiently by prioritising tasks.

Figure 3.6 A variety of operating systems: Windows 7, Android, Ubuntu and Mac OS X. Each OS is appropriate for the hardware system it runs on.

Activity: Comparing operating systems

Weblink

1 Follow the weblink from the *Digital Technologies 9 & 10* website to the Internet Archives page where you will find a recreation of Apple's operating system for the Macintosh computer from 1991.
2 What are your first impressions using this 1991 operating system?

3 Complete the table below (you can copy it to a spreadsheet) comparing this early GUI with two other contemporary ones. Add additional features.

4 Try out some of the early games provided when you are finished!

Table 3.1

Feature	Mac System 7 (1991)	Current Apple OS	Current Windows OS
Appearance			
File handling			
Interaction with peripheral devices			

The fetch-execute cycle

The machine cycle is at the heart of what happens inside a computer.

To run a computer program loaded into RAM, the CPU repeats the same cycle for every instruction it receives. There are four steps to the machine cycle (Figure 3.7):

- **Fetch:** read an instruction stored in memory (RAM).
- **Decode:** translate the instruction.
- **Execute:** perform the instruction.
- **Store:** write the result to memory (RAM).

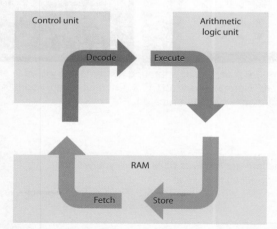

Figure 3.7 The machine cycle and the main components involved at each stage.

Parts of a CPU

First we need to identify the CPU parts, which all work together to perform a machine cycle:

- **Program counter (PC):** Holds the address of the instruction to be executed next.
- **Address register:** Holds the address of a block of memory.
- **Data register:** A register that holds data coming from or going to memory
- **Instruction register (IR):** A temporary holding space for an instruction that has just been fetched from memory.
- **Control unit (CU):** Decodes the program instruction in the IR, selects arithmetic and logic operations, and coordinates.
- **Arithmetic logic unit (ALU):** Performs mathematical and logical operations.
- **Floating-point unit (FPU):** Performs floating-point operations.

Class activity: What do you know already?

In small groups select one question from the list below, agree on an answer and share with the class.

- What sort of tasks are computers good at? Recall how computers beat humans at certain jobs – which jobs are these?
- How does a computer keep track of the instructions it is executing?
- What does 'gigahertz' mean when referring to CPUs?
- Which hardware components act as a computer's short-term and long-term memory?

Making sense of the machine cycle

Let's say you wrote this program to add two integers, A and B:

```
A = 3
B = 4
C = A + B
```

When this program runs on a computer, at the lowest level we would see high and low voltages on the many wires connected to the CPU chip (see Figure 3.8). These would switch on and off and signal to the chip which actions it needs to perform.

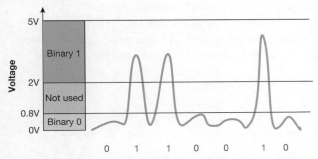

Figure 3.8 Binary is represented in a digital system using voltages. A binary 1 is usually represented by any voltage between 2V to 5V and a binary 0 by any voltage between 0V and 0.8V.

The program itself would be stored in the working memory of the computer (RAM) as binary data.

Translated into binary machine language our three-line program might look like:

```
0110010000000011
0100000000000100
0010100000001010
```

… not very helpful to humans!

Information in the memory of the computer is in two parts: instructions and data.

Using an invented human-readable language known as assembly language we could write this as follows. Here the letters are instructions and the numbers are data:

```
LOD-C 3
ADD-C 4
STO 10
HLT
```

LOD, ADD, STO and HLT are made-up acronyms, which mean Load, Add, Store and Halt.

Table 3.2 explains each line of this code.

Table 3.2 Our small program in assembly language, adding 3 and 4 together.

Memory location	Instruction	Data	Meaning
0	LOD-C	3	Load a constant number 3 into the accumulator
1	ADD-C	4	Add a constant number 4 to whatever is in the accumulator
2	STO	10	Write whatever data is in the accumulator to memory location 10
3	HLT		Stop execution of the program

This program has to be loaded one instruction at a time from RAM memory into the CPU of the computer where all the work is done.

Three major sections of the CPU work together to achieve this:

- registers (address register, program counter, instruction register, data registers and accumulator)
- ALU
- control.

All these march to the drum beat of a built-in clock, ticking at millions of times per second. This speed is described as the clock speed of the computer. These days a typical clock speed is around 3 Ghz, which is 3 billion cycles per second.

All data are loaded into the main memory (RAM) and the CPU can start its machine cycles.

Understanding the detail

Referring to Table 3.2 above, we will examine just the second line in our code in detail.

1 Fetch or read the next instruction

The *program counter* is pointing to the first address in memory to be processed. We will imagine we are at the second line in our example. This instruction is made up of two parts and looks like this:

```
ADD-C 4
```

The first part is the operation code (opcode) ADD-C, which tells the computer what to do with the second part, the operand 4.

The instruction part is sent to the instruction register and the address part (if there is one) is sent to the address register. Here there is no address as we are using the actual integer value of 4.

The program counter now points to the next instruction, keeping track of where the program is up to, ready later for the next cycle.

9780170411820

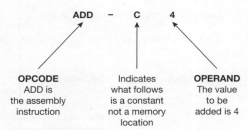

ADD – C 4

OPCODE
ADD is
the assembly
instruction

Indicates
what follows
is a constant
not a memory
location

OPERAND
The value
to be
added is 4

Figure 3.9 The anatomy of an assembly code program instruction

2 Decode instruction

The opcode instruction ADD-C is decoded by the control unit (CU). Here the meaning is: 'load the operand as an integer constant into the accumulator'.

Each different CPU understands only its own set of commands, called its instruction set, and different computers use different CPUs.

This decoding step lets the CU know what operands it needs to fetch from memory.

3 Read the address

If there is a memory address to deal with, this is now read. In our example, there isn't one. If there was it would look like ADD 5.

4 Execute the instruction

The instruction is performed – the main step from a user's point of view. If the instruction is arithmetic or logic then the ALU is used. In our example, ADD-C involves two steps.

In the first step the operand 4 is added by the ALU to the number already stored there (it was 3 in the last cycle for LOD-C) in the accumulator.

In the second step, the result 7 is sent back to the accumulator, wiping out any previous value stored, while the CPU increments the program counter.

This step can also often be just a single step, as in the case of a simple LOAD or STORE instruction.

Activity: Seeing the cycle in action!

A simulated CPU

In 1995 David Ecks wrote a wonderful book called *The Most Complex Machine*, which explains how a computer works from start to finish.

Accompanying this book is a set of small programs available online. One of these is xComputer, which simulates the working CPU of a computer. xComputer lets you load programs and data into the memory of a simulated CPU and watch while the machine cycles run. To simplify the steps, the program displays only the registers, the clock cycle and the main memory (RAM). You will have to believe the ALU adds and that control is doing its job behind the scenes!

Watching a CPU in action

The xComputer app will allow you to watch your assembly language code in action (see Figure 3.10).

Using the Step button you will be able to follow each stage of the fetch-execute cycle explained above. Here's how:

1 For instructions on accessing this software go to the weblink on our online resources page.
   Click the link *xComputer.jar* within the Applet Jar Files (software) section of the website and select the browser option to open or run the applet. You can also download a stand-alone version of the program.

2 Select 'Instructions' from the drop-down menu (see Figure 3.11).

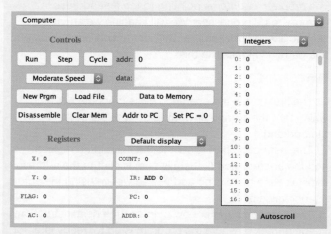

Figure 3.10 The xComputer interface

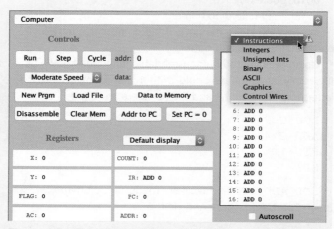

Figure 3.11 The xComputer interface. Set the drop-down menu to Instructions.

3 Click the 'New Prgm' button. An empty window appears.

9780170411820

4   We will now write the code for adding our two integers, 3 and 4, together. Type these four lines of assembly code (see Figure 3.12) into the empty window. Note that you can name and save the program using Save to File.

```
LOD-C 3
ADD-C 4
STO 10
HLT
```

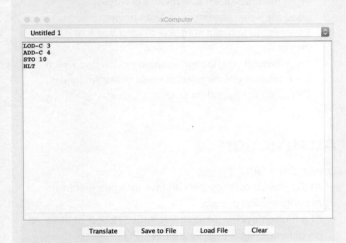

Figure 3.12 The assembly code program typed into xComputer to add integers 3 and 4.

5   Press the Translate button. You will see the program loaded into memory and the CPU interface as shown in Figure 3.13. Make sure 'Instructions' is showing in the top right corner drop-down as shown.

6   Set up a separate spreadsheet file using Excel or Google Sheets as shown in Table 3.3. Copy the layout shown and record changing values at each step.

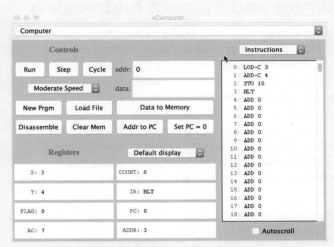

Figure 3.13 xComputer showing the program loaded in memory

7   Fill in the values in your spreadsheet as you repeatedly press 'Step' and watch as the fetch-execute cycle steps through its cycles.

8   Complete the Cycle phase row by naming the fetch-execute phase for each clock step: either fetch, decode, execute or store. Note that not all instructions include a store phase. A yellow flash in the xComputer applet display indicates each step in the store phase (e.g. at the end of the STO 10 instruction).

9   Re-run the program: Set PC=0 and click 'Run', trying out various speeds using the drop-down menu or it may be best to quit the application and reload your saved assembly code.

10 Re-run the program: Set PC=0 and click 'Cycle', to see what happens at the end of each cycle.

Table 3.3 The layout for your spreadsheet to record changing values during the fetch-execute cycle.

CPU component	Clock cycle:	1	1	1	1	1	1	2	2	etc.
	Clock step:	1	2	3	4	5	6	1	2	etc.
	Cycle phase									
COUNT	Counter									
IR	Instruction register									
PC	Program counter									
ADDR	Current address									
X	X register									
Y	Y register									
AC	Accumulator									

Activity: CPU cycle play reading

The CPU cycle comes to life in a bonus activity included as part of the online resources for this chapter.

Direct and indirect addressing

The previous activity used what is known as *direct addressing*.

LOD-C 4 means 'load integer 4'. It treats whatever follows as a constant.

A second, more common type of addressing is known as *indirect addressing*. Our assembly instruction for this is simply LOD.

LOD 4 will load any data in memory location 4 into the accumulator. These different meanings are important.

Here is our previous program again using indirect addressing. Here 4 and 5 are memory locations, not values:

```
LOD  4
ADD  5
STO  10
HLT
3
4
```

Memory location 4 is storing the integer 3, and location 5 is storing the integer 4. What each line does now is outlined in Table 3.4:

Table 3.4

Memory location	Instruction	Data	Meaning
0	LOD	4	Load data from memory location 4 into the accumulator
1	ADD	5	Load data from memory location 5 into the accumulator
2	STO	10	Write accumulator data to memory location 10
3	HLT		Stop execution of the program
4		3	Integer 3 is stored here at memory location 4
5		4	Integer 4 is stored here at memory location 5

Web probe: xComputer

1 Open the stand-alone version of the program.
2 Select 'Instructions' from the drop-down menu (see Figure 3.13).
3 Click 'New Program'.
4 Type this version of the code to add integers 3 and 4 indirectly from memory locations at 4 and 5.
5 Click 'Step' to watch the fetch-execute cycle and complete a second spreadsheet, using the layout of Table 3.4 as a guide, to record the values at each step. Note that the final result of 7 will appear at memory location 10. Explain why.

Activity: What's really going on?

You may have wondered how the CPU knows what parts of its chip should be turned on or off to perform each instruction. This is achieved by an even lower level language, at the level of the circuitry known as microinstructions.

If you want to see what really happens at the circuitry level when your program is run, xComputer even allows you to do this!

1 From the drop-down select Control wires.
2 Load the same assembly code as before.
3 Press PC=0 to make sure you are pointing to the first instruction.
4 Step through your loaded assembly code and watch how different combination of wires of our (imaginary) CPU chip are turned on or off.

Abstraction

Levels of the CPU:

- At the lowest level of the CPU we imagine electrons moving around circuits.
- At a higher level we imagine voltages raised or lowered on different wires to operate the CPU.
- At a higher level still we imagine our code represented as binary digits (bits).
- At an even higher level we represent the binary using assembly language to make it easier for us to understand.
- At the highest level as programmers we write our code in languages such as Python, C++, JavaScript and so on.

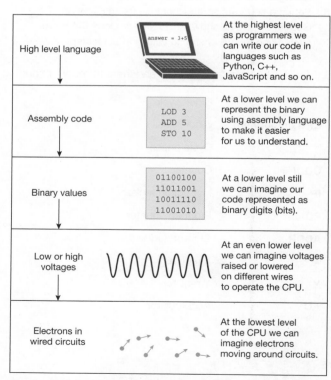

Figure 3.14 Levels of abstraction in understanding a computer

If we had to think about all this when coding, no one could code! The lower realities are hidden from us when we code. We certainly don't think at the level of electrons running around circuits.

The only code a computer can execute is called machine code or **object code** and is often represented in binary. This is produced by compilers (or assemblers) from assembly language. Code written by humans is in higher level human-readable programming languages and uses ordinary text. This is called **source code**.

Writing code in a higher level language, such as Python, is called abstraction. It is the important principle in computational thinking we learnt in *Digital Technologies 7 & 8*. Abstraction turns something complex into something simpler by removing detail and reducing it to a general principle or main idea. It is the third stage in computational thinking.

REVIEW

Identify

1 Three terms are commonly used to describe a computer's CPU cycles while executing a program. What are they?

_____

_____

2 What is the purpose of the CPU in a computer?

_____

_____

3 Explain the main task of each the following components in the CPU.

a Control

_____

_____

b RAM

_____

_____

c Address register

_____

_____

d Program counter register

_____

_____

e Instruction register

_____

_____

f ALU

_____

_____

g Accumulator

_____

_____

9780170411820

4 Explain what source code is.

_____

_____

_____

5 Explain what assembly language is.

_____

_____

_____

Analyse

6 What is the difference between direct and indirect memory addressing?

_____

_____

_____

7 Outline the four basic stages of the CPU fetch-execute cycle.

_____

_____

_____

_____

_____

_____

Research

8 The specifications for the speed of a computer might be 2 or 3 Ghz. However, other factors may affect its actual performance. Use Internet research to find out what at least five of these other factors might be.

_____

_____

_____

9 Complete the table comparing the major technical specifications of your own and another computer you have access to.

Table 3.5

Specification	My computer	Another computer
The amount of RAM memory		
The speed and generation of your CPU (the system clock)		
The size of the registers (word size) on your CPU		
The bus type and speed		
Input and output devices		
The amount of cache memory		

UNDERSTANDING ISSUES

OUTCOMES

Australian curriculum content descriptions:

- Define and decompose real-world problems taking into account functional requirements and economic, environmental, social, technical and usability constraints (ACTDIP027) (AC)
- Evaluate how student solutions and existing information systems meet needs, are innovative, and take account of future risks and sustainability (ACTDIP031) (AC)
- Develop techniques for acquiring, storing and validating quantitative and qualitative data from a range of sources, considering privacy and security requirements (ACTDIP036) (AC)
- Define and decompose real-world problems precisely, taking into account functional and non-functional requirements and including interviewing stakeholders to identify needs (ACTDIP038) (AC)
- Evaluate critically how student solutions and existing information systems and policies, take account of future risks and sustainability and provide opportunities for innovation and enterprise (ACTDIP042) (AC)
- Create interactive solutions for sharing ideas and information online, taking into account safety, social contexts and legal responsibilities (ACTDIP043) (AC)
- Plan and manage projects using an iterative and collaborative approach, identifying risks and considering safety and sustainability (ACTDIP044) (AC)

GLOSSARY

accessibility The degree to which a system is designed to maximise access and use by people with disabilities

digital footprint A record of the complete data resulting from a person's use of a digital system

equity The principle that all people should have equal right of access to information technologies

ethics The moral principles that guide a person's behaviour

Developers of technology solutions have not always taken responsibility for the impacts their work will have.

In the projects you undertake in this course, you are expected to consider the social, ethical and legal impacts of the solutions you produce.

SOCIAL ISSUES

Information and software technology has altered the nature of work and enterprise to the extent that most jobs in the developed world now involve computers. How will society change as we rely more and more on computers and automated systems rather than interacting directly with people?

Many new jobs have been created as a result of new technologies; for example, database administrators, social media managers and web designers. However, some jobs have been made redundant. Travel agents, for example, have been significantly affected by technology. Many people now prefer to research and book their own travel plans online without the assistance of a travel agent.

In your lifetime you can expect to witness many social changes due to technology. Do you think the next decade will involve as much change as the past decade?

Web probe: The Industrial Revolution and the Internet revolution

The arrival of the Internet brought about the world's biggest social change since Europe's Industrial Revolution of the 18th to 19th centuries.

1 Use the Internet to research what caused the Industrial Revolution. Next, research the ways it effected society.

2 Use the information to create and complete a table by first identifying a change and then deciding if you believe change was good, bad or neither, by using an X in the appropriate column.

3 Finally, as a class work collaboratively with a single copy of this table and see how many different entries can be collected by adding rows as needed. Use Google Sheets or a similar online collaborative tool.

Table 4.1

Industrial Revolution					Internet revolution			
Change	Good	Bad	Neither		Change	Good	Bad	Neither

The benefits of technology – such as instant communication and social networking – must be balanced against reduced personal contact.

Figure 4.1

Figure 4.2

Explain what you think these two Michael Leunig cartoons (Figures 4.1 and 4.2) are saying and write a personal response outlining both positive and negative effects of the Internet on society.

_____

_____

_____

_____

_____

_____

_____

_____

_____

Knowledge probe: Facebook and fake news

After initially denying there was a problem, in 2017 Facebook said it was implementing measures to combat false news stories posted on its site intended to sway public opinion.

Printed newspapers are struggling with low circulations and some have ceased publication. Important news stories appear in social media such as Twitter and Facebook before they appear in mainstream media. The only news some people receive is via social media sites. False stories have been credited with swaying American voters in presidential elections.

One central issue raised by these facts is *curation*.

1 Find out what a curator does in an art gallery.
2 How do traditional printed encyclopedias curate their information?

_____

_____

_____

3 How does Wikipedia curate its information?

_____

_____

_____

4 Do Twitter or Facebook have curation?

_____

5 What is algorithmic curation?

_____

_____

_____

_____

_____

9780170411820

6 Recently Facebook offered to improve its algorithmic curation after it featured a number of fake news items on its news feed. Would you trust algorithmic curation?

_____

_____

_____

_____

THE WAY WE PLAY: CONSUMERS OR CREATORS?

Video-game players' faces were secretly captured by Robbie Cooper in a video project he called 'Immersion'. Follow the weblink from the _Digital Technologies 9 & 10_ website to watch the video.
Video

It has been argued that many young people grow up as 'screen kids' who only become consumers of technology and not creators. What is your view?

_____

_____

_____

_____

_____

_____

_____

_____

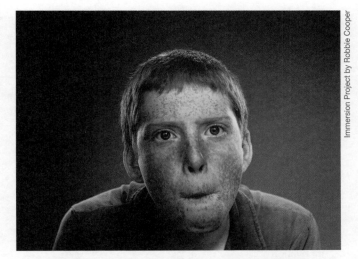
Immersion Project by Robbie Cooper

Figure 4.3 Faces of video-game players

THE WAY WE WORK

Not so long ago, the only people who looked for 'gigs' were musicians; now many make their living by working gigs rather than working full time.

The term 'gig economy' describes how digital technology has made it possible for anyone to offer goods and services over the Internet using computers and GPS enabled smartphones. The earliest examples were computer programmers and designers accepting short-term work as freelancers. Now millions of entrepreneurs sell their products through Etsy, offer short-term accommodation through Airbnb, hire cars using Uber and even teachers offer lesson plans through TpT.

1 List five examples of the gig economy not included in the examples on page 33.

_____

_____

_____

_____

_____

_____

2 One of the earliest examples of the gig economy was Elance. Describe what it was and what it is now. Find an Australian equivalent.

_____

3 The introduction of digital technologies has meant big changes in employment. Table 4.2 lists some of the issues raised by the 'gig economy'. Suggest both good and bad outcomes for each.

Table 4.2

Impact on	Good outcome	Bad outcome
Entrepreneurism		
Types of jobs		
Innovation		
Income		
Job security		
Consumer guarantees		
Work from home		
Family life		
Worker interaction		
Company monopolies		
Social welfare		
Workplace health and safety		
Pay rates		
Shared documents in the cloud		
Training		

THE WAY WE SHOP

It is now possible to buy almost anything online. This has impacted physical retailers greatly and the trend promises to continue. In 2017 Amazon announced it was setting up a warehouse in Australia. Analysts believe that both bricks-and-mortar and online retailers will be affected by this arrival.

Activity: Amazon

Use Table 4.3 to list five potential impacts arising from an Australian-based Amazon warehouse.

Table 4.3

Impact on	Good outcome	Bad outcome

INFOBIT: HOW LONG IS TOO LONG?

According to survey data of 10 billion users of online shopping sites, if a web page takes longer than three seconds to load, half the shoppers will have left and a delay of 100 milliseconds means 7% of potential sales will be lost.

THE WAY WE TREAT OUR WORLD

Where do computers go when they die?

In the West African nation of Ghana, a huge e-waste dump called Agbogbloshie lies alongside the now highly polluted main river, the Odaw, its banks littered with millions of discarded electronic waste parts. Children scavenge through the poisonous rubbish, burning circuit-boards over open fires to melt out the tin, gold and lead, breathing in the toxic fumes, earning less than a dollar a day.

Old computers never die – they just pollute our environment for a long time. Computer equipment becomes old very quickly. The life expectancy of a computer purchased today is only about three years.

How many old computers, monitors and printers are lying around your home? If the whole class was asked and

Figure 4.4 Disposal of old computers and peripheral equipment involves solving the challenging issues of recycling and disposal of toxic wastes.

the number of unused pieces of equipment totalled, what do you think the total would come to?

Visit Greenpeace International and research e-waste

Every year, millions of old computers are buried in land fill and start immediately to pollute our soil as they contain hazardous wastes such as lead and other metals. Some companies offer recycling services. After the leaded glass is removed from monitors and melted down, the rest of the equipment is often sent overseas so that parts with value can be stripped.

Although we may feel positive after recycling our equipment, often we have just shifted the pollution to another place on the globe.

In Ghana and in China, mountains of hardware arrive by truck, tractor and even bicycle. Because labour is cheap, the work of removing the wiring and separating the plastic from the metal components is done by hand.

The wiring removed during the day forms huge piles from which the insulation is removed simply by burning it through the night. This action produces ash loaded with dioxins and releases toxic compounds into the air, which become part of the air we breathe. Valueless parts are often dumped. Old glass and plastic fill irrigation ditches and chemicals leach into rivers.

Microchips have metal pins with small amounts of gold plating and, in a process similar to the worst days of early gold mining, they are left to dissolve in vats of acid to collect tiny amounts of gold. Fumes fill the air and the residue is tipped as slurry onto the ground and pollutes groundwater.

Perhaps it would be preferable for us to fill our garages with old equipment rather than recycle it until better methods emerge. Maybe the real solution is for manufacturers to be given responsibility by governments for the proper disposal of their equipment after it becomes obsolete. Better still, they could be encouraged to build equipment with fewer hazardous materials.

As a class decide the top three environmental issues in digital technology. Record these along with actions you believe would help in Table 4.4.

Table 4.4

Issue	Response

In a survey, people were asked to decide the issues they thought digital technologies might one day be able to solve. The unordered survey responses are listed in Table 4.5.

1   Form a group and re-order the responses with most likely (for technology to be able to solve) at the top to least likely at the bottom. Are any issues already being solved using technology?

2   Next, order them into two piles: likely to be solved, unlikely to be solved.

3   Collect the number of votes from the class for items voted 'likely to be solved' from step 2 and record this data in a spreadsheet. Create a pie chart using this data.

4   Finish comparing answers as a class and discussing what makes some issues hard or easy to solve by using technology.

5   Now compare your results with those of the official survey by using a spreadsheet. Go to the *Digital Technologies 9 & 10* website to view the survey data in the PDF 'What problems can technology solve?'.

6   **Optional extra:** Design a shared online database and have each person in the class enter a score against each item from 1 (easy for technology to solve) to 5 (impossible for technology to solve). How close is this outcome to your group's conclusions?

Table 4.5

Waste treatment	Soil quality	Famine
Beach and river pollution	Threat of nuclear war	Domestic violence
Contamination of food	Terrorism	Racism
Air pollution	Bullying	Over population
Refugees	Car accidents	Homelessness
Ozone depletion	Land salinity	Street violence
Climate change	Unemployment	Species extinction

ETHICAL ISSUES

Ethics are standards or moral principles that guide people and organisations in what is the right behaviour.

When a scammer imitates a banking website with a false message attempting to steal personal details, all of us would agree this is wrong ethically, and possibly legally. However, when a legal software download site carries ad buttons designed to look like the download button to trick users, is this unethical or just smart business practice? See Figure 4.5.

Codes of conduct

Although not legally enforceable, codes of conduct are rules which guide organisations in ethical behaviour.

A well-known example is Facebook's age limit of at least 13 years old for account holders.

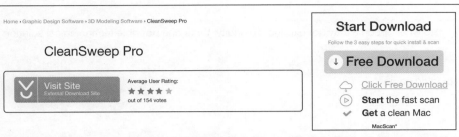

Figure 4.5 The user wanted to download CleanSweep Pro, but this 'free download' button is really a hyperlink to an advertisement for another product.

Privacy

Privacy is the right of any person or group to keep their lives from public view and to have control over who sees it. Sometimes an action that breaches privacy might not be illegal but is unethical.

Examples of breaches of privacy range from when someone tags another person's photo without their permission to displaying a photo of a deceased person of Aboriginal or Torres Strait Islander descent.

Digital footprints

In the digital age we provide far more information about ourselves than we might imagine. The glossary for Digital Technologies for the Australian Curriculum describes our **digital footprints** comprehensively this way:

> A person's *digital footprint* includes all information actively provided by that person such as interactions on social networks (for example, comments, photographs), online purchases, website logons, emails and instant messages. It also includes passive information such as logs of software installed and used on a computer, metadata associated with files, a user's IP address, a device being used to access a web page, and a user's browsing history stored as cookies or by Internet service providers.
>
> ACARA, 2016, Digital Technologies for the Australian Curriculum

Others can find out a lot more about you than you might imagine! Your journeys by public transport can be tracked from your transport card if your identity is linked to it by bank details.

Many people, young and old, have failed to win job interviews because the personal information they unwittingly made public on social media sites disqualified them in the eyes of their prospective employers.

A number of the projects in the data analysis and visualisation section illustrate these privacy concerns.

Equity and the right of access

Equal employment opportunity (EEO) legislation requires, for example, women, Indigenous Australians and people with a disability to be given fair access to employment.

Workplace health and safety (WHS) legislation requires every workplace in Australia to ensure rules and training are established for a safe working environment.

For those working in digital technologies, it is often easier to provide equal opportunity than in many other workplace situations.

Figure 4.6 Anti-discrimination legislation aims to create an environment where people are judged on their abilities and not treated unfairly because of other factors such as age, marital status, race or disability.

Equity refers to the principle that all people should have *equal right of access* to information technologies. Unfortunately, not all people have this access. Some may not be able to afford it. Some people may have difficulty with movement, eyesight or hearing due to a disability. Some may lack Internet access because they live in an isolated community.

Activity: Equity

1 Table 4.6 lists examples where people may not experience equity. Write one possible technological solution for each case.

Table 4.6

Child not understanding game instructions	
Poor eyesight	
Poor hearing	
Inability to afford a computer	
Person lacking confidence using technology	
Disability with lack of dexterity	

2 **Accessibility** is a word used in information technology to describe the need for as many people as possible to be able to access technology. Use the Internet to research efforts in this area by combining the word 'accessibility' with a manufacturer's name, such as Apple, Microsoft, Samsung and Google in your search.
Compare the accessibility policies of these large companies.

3 The latest Mac and Windows versions of Microsoft Word include a Check Accessibility tool under the Revew tab. Open a reasonably long Word document and try it out.
How useful was this check?

9780170411820

LEGAL ISSUES

Many issues fall under more than one category. For example, privacy issues are only legal issues if a law is broken. Many breaches of privacy may not break the law but can be extremely serious invasions of a person's right to privacy.

Here we consider some of these issues.

Knowledge probe: A hidden web

A big concern in society is the way governments and other organisations can discover personal details by connecting information from a number of separate sources.

Give three examples of how unintended information could be discovered by connecting data in the databases shown in Figure 4.7.

Knowledge
Probe

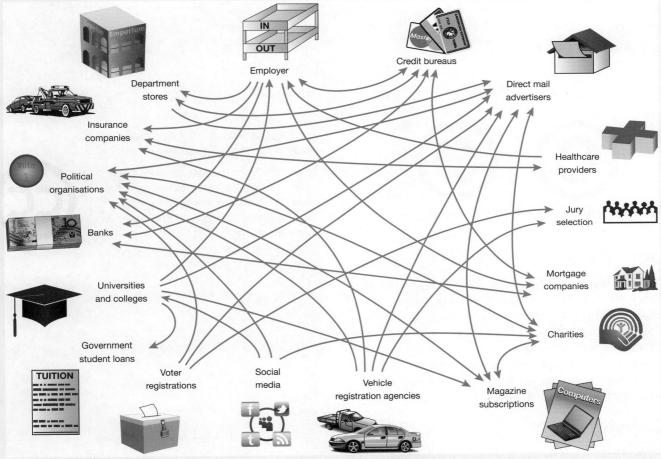

Figure 4.7 When an organisation acquires data, it is sometimes shared with other organisations without users being informed.

_____

_____

_____

_____

_____

_____

Search the Internet for 'World's biggest data breaches'. Select three cases where privacy of users was breached and briefly describe the event, how it is thought to have occurred and the number of users affected.

Table 4.7

Year	Description	How	Number of users

Figure 4.8 Copyright and copyleft symbols

Shutterstock.com/Miceking

Copyright

Copyright is your right to own the intellectual property you create. You have the right to control its reproduction by others and the right to seek reward for its use by others.

When software, music or movies are downloaded illegally, the downloader is stealing.

In Australia, copyright lasts for 70 years after the death of its creator. Copyright law is defined by the Australian Copyright Act of 1968.

Copyleft

Copyleft is a form of licencing in which creators offer people the right to freely reproduce, distribute and modify a work as long as the same rights are applied to the copies (i.e. you cannot restrict usage).

Creative Commons licences do not replace copyright law but are based on it. When you use Google search tools for images and select 'Usage rights' you will see four alternative choices listed after the default setting. You need to know what each of these four choices means if you use these images in your projects.

List and explain each of these here.

Figure 4.9

Shutterstock.com/Icons vector

Table 4.8

Usage	Explanation

Class activity: Taking a stand

Figure 4.10 Taking a stand on issues

1   Your teacher will attach to opposite walls of the classroom two large labels, containing the words 'Agree' and 'Disagree' with an open space in the centre.

2   Someone is chosen as announcer. As each statement is read aloud by the announcer, each student takes a position somewhere on an imaginary line drawn between the two walls. If they completely agree, they touch the 'Agree' wall; if undecided, they stand in the middle of the room; if they disagree strongly, they touch the 'Disagree' wall. (Imagine the numbers 1 to 5 across a line from wall to wall where 1 is complete agreement, 3 is undecided and 5 is complete disagreement).

Students take any position across the room depending upon their reaction to the statement.

If you are the only student standing at one extreme, it might be because you interpreted the question completely differently – so don't allow yourself to be bullied into following the crowd! Some statements are designed to trap!

Each statement is read out, going to the next one only when everyone is standing still. Any person may ask for an explanation of any statement, but at this stage no debate is allowed. If unclear about a statement, stand in the middle.

3   The teacher records the results of each question by noting roughly where most of the class stood. The teacher identifies the issues that split the class most. The class then decides which issues they would most like to discuss.

4   Small groups form for each topic and elect a notekeeper, with 5–10 minutes for discussion.

Table 4.9

Issue	1	2	3	4	5
Use the columns to record approximate numbers where 1 represents strong agreement and 5 represents strong disagreement.					
Learning computing as a subject should be compulsory in school					
Elections should be conducted electronically					
Within our lifetimes cars will have the ability to be guided electronically to their destination					
We would have more unemployment if computers did not exist					
If I knew that a technological invention of mine would one day be used to create a weapon, I would keep it secret					
The Internet should not be controlled by the government					
It is okay for children to have uncensored Internet access at home					
The Internet should be subject to censorship					
The government should make Internet sites that describe how to perform acts of terrorism illegal					
Schools should censor Internet access					
The government should keep database records confidential					
Companies such as Google should refuse to conduct business in countries which censor their search engines or users' emails					
Daily newspapers in printed form will cease to exist in my lifetime					
Government agencies should be permitted to join databases together (aggregate) to track activity					
Private companies should be permitted to share information on customers with one another					
To prevent false identity and control illegal activity it should be acceptable for governments to allow electronic identification chips to be embedded in our bodies at birth					
School records should follow us electronically through our lives and be available to employers and government					
It is acceptable for our buying habits to be recorded by marketing agencies					
Smartphone manufacturers should provide governments with the ability to access their products in the case of suspected illegal activity					
Wealthy nations should provide technology to poorer nations					

Identify

1 Identify three social issues in digital technology.

_____

2 Identify three ethical issues in digital technology.

_____

3 Identify three legal issues in digital technology.

_____

Analyse

4 Discuss two effects of digital technology on employment.

_____

_____

_____

_____

5 Identify one example of an issue of accessibility in digital technology that you have witnessed and suggest a solution.

_____

_____

_____

_____

Research

6 You have been commissioned by the federal government to propose a five-point plan to address the problem of e-waste. Develop five points and briefly justify each one.

_____

_____

_____

_____

_____

_____

7 Research the techniques Facebook uses to identify false news posted on its site. Suggest how these techniques might work and state how reliable you think they might be.

_____

_____

_____

_____

_____

UNDERSTANDING PROJECT MANAGEMENT: DOCUMENTATION AND BACKUPS

05

OUTCOMES

Australian curriculum content descriptions:
- Plan and manage projects using an iterative and collaborative approach, identifying risks and considering safety and sustainability (ACTDIP032) **AC**
- Create interactive solutions for sharing ideas and information online, taking into account safety, social contexts and legal responsibilities (ACTDIP043) **AC**
- Plan and manage projects using an iterative and collaborative approach, identifying risks and considering safety and sustainability (ACTDIP044) **AC**

content descriptions

GLOSSARY

backup Copying and archiving computer data so it may be used to restore original data after corruption or loss

Gantt chart Horizontal coloured bars that represent planned and actual dates the various tasks in a project are to be completed

project An individual or group activity intended to achieve a stated goal or identified need that proceeds in organised stages such as defining, designing, implementing and evaluating

project management Overall oversight and control of planning, monitoring and execution of a project. The critical feature of project management is the successful achievement of the stated outcomes within budget and within time

versioning A documentation process that records stages in software development so as to distinguish between versions and identify the latest revision

In Chapter 5: Understanding project management in *Digital Technologies 7 & 8* we learnt the stages through which a typical **project** travels before it is complete. We learnt that in many cases this design cycle repeats and usually is never complete!

In this chapter we will examine two other important **project management** processes: documentation and **backup**.

THE IMPORTANCE OF DOCUMENTATION

There will be many times in your life where you will need to work alongside others as part of a project. It may be establishing a new business, renovating a house or planning a trip.

In the same way, it is very unusual for software these days to be the work of just one person. Software is just too complex and requires specialised skills such as managers, interface designers, creative artists, audio engineers, video producers, animators, programmers, analysts, quality control testers and a sales and marketing team.

If a critical member of the team leaves for some reason, the person replacing them will need to know what they have done and why and what they were planning to do next.

In addition, the whole team needs to keep to a deadline for delivery of the working product.

Types of documentation

The most successful project teams have excellent communication skills and methods. These involve verbal, written and visual communication methods. These are all forms of documentation.

Verbal documentation

It is very common for each member of the team to have a completely different picture of the same project – even though they are working on it together!

The project leader needs to be able to clarify the purpose of a project and set a common goal all members understand and share. Also, team members need to be able to explain their ideas clearly to the project leader.

Written documentation

Have you ever tried to understand code written by someone else?

If they have not made written comments throughout their code then this can be almost impossible.

Skill builder: Clear communication

1 Select one of the images in Figure 5.1 and describe it to the class so that they can draw the image. You must not use geometric shape names (e.g. you cannot say 'rectangle').

2 When finished, everyone holds up their efforts while you point out drawings that pass the test.

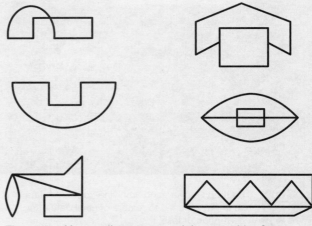

Figure 5.1 How well can you explain something?

3 Were you successful at getting others to draw an acceptable shape?

_____

4 Write down what you learnt from this activity.

_____

_____

_____

_____

_____

_____

5 How can a project leader make sure they are clear when using verbal instructions?

_____

_____

_____

_____

9780170411820

INFOBIT: THE Y2K CRISIS

In the years and months leading up to the year 2000 (Y2K), analysts started to find that some software systems were showing faults in calculations that involved the year 2000. They realised that this was due to computer systems storing the year portion of dates in two digits – 00 – and these dates were being interpreted as the year 1900 rather than 2000.

Billions of dollars were spent because older programs had no documentation and were very hard for even experienced programmers to locate the code they needed to fix.

As the clock ticked over for the millennium's New Year, fireworks exploded, crowds cheered, almost nothing failed but the world could have saved lots of money if programs had included clear documentation.

A good programmer will add lots of comments. These are not part of the code itself. They will also use variables that have meaning, such as using the word *counter* instead of x for how many times a program's loop is executed.

Here is an example of a program containing comment documentation. Normally only parts of the program that need explanation will have comments. The different colours used for computer code words are another form of program documentation as they distinguish between variables, functions, strings and keywords.

Versioning

Many software projects are completed by online teams whose members work collaboratively using shared documents online. As a software project progresses it is important to keep track of past versions as well as clearly identifying the current working version. If team members are in different time zones then agreement needs to be reached on how times should be recorded.

Versioning is a documentation process that usually uses decimal numbers to record stages in project development.

Major updates have a change in the first number and smaller changes are indicated by additional numbers separated by full stops.

Table 5.1

Version	Comment
0.9.1	Version for in-house development
0.9.2	Improved in-house prototype
1.0	First major release
1.0.5	Minor updates to major release
1.0.6	Very small update in release version
2.0	Major update

```
#This program plays the game of HiLo. User guesses secret integer
#import maths module needed to generate secret integer
import random
#generate random integer secret: 1 ≤ secret ≤ 100
secret = random.randint(1,100)
#print while testing only
print (secret)
#set flag to allow repeated guessing
flag = True
while flag == True:
  guess = input ('Your guess?: ')
  #guess is string, so convert to integer
  guess = int (guess)
  # print suitable messages
  if guess < secret:
    print ('Too low')
  elif guess > secret:
    print ('Too high')
  else:
    print ('Correct!')
    #set flag when correct guess
    flag = False
```

Figure 5.2 Examples of internal program documentation

ReadMe, changelogs, licences and bug listings

A ReadMe file should give general information about a project. It should be in plain text format (not a Word file or pdf). It should contain a few lines explaining the purpose of the project and information about authors. Often a short summary of the changes in the code over time is included (a changelog) and a list of known bugs that need fixing.

A licence file describes the conditions under which the software is made available to the public.

Meeting minutes

Project teams need to have meetings regularly and notes called 'minutes' need to be recorded so that any misunderstandings over decisions can be checked.

Visual documentation

Mind maps and brainstorming

Generating ideas can be a creative and spontaneous. It is useful to document ideas to revisit them later or share them with others. You might choose to use a concept map (see Figure 5.3). There are computer programs, such as FreeMind®, that can help you to draw these diagrams.

Charts

Figure 5.4 is an example of how a chart can help plan a website, showing links and the navigation plan. In this case it is in the form of a sitemap.

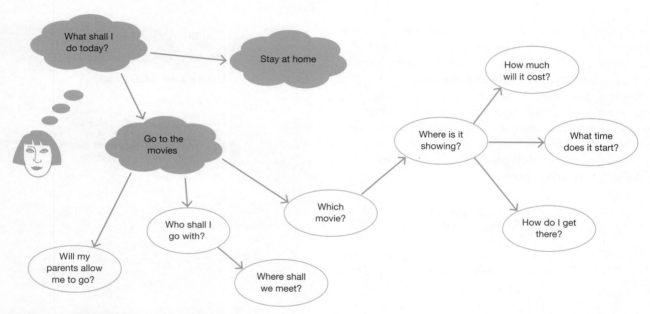

Figure 5.3 Brainstorming a trip to the movies

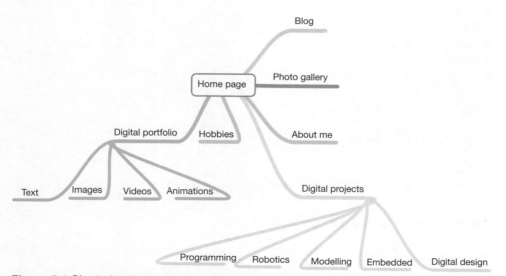

Figure 5.4 Chart showing navigation for a planned student website

9780170411820

Flowcharts

We learnt about flowcharts as a form of documentation in *Digital Technologies 7 & 8*. An example flowchart for the program in Figure 5.2 appears in Figure 5.5 below.

Timelines and financial plans

Perhaps the most important pieces of visual documentation for large projects are timelines and financial plans.

A timeline is often called a **Gantt chart** (see Figure 5.6). It shows horizontal coloured bars that represent the dates various tasks in a large project are to be ready. A second bar tracks progress during each task.

Financial plans are spreadsheets that show planned and actual costs of the components of the project.

Other forms of documentation

Tutorials, walkthroughs, getting started, user manuals, FAQ (Frequently Asked Questions) and troubleshooting guides are all other examples of important documentation.

Include in your plans for projects the appropriate documentation that needs to be produced.

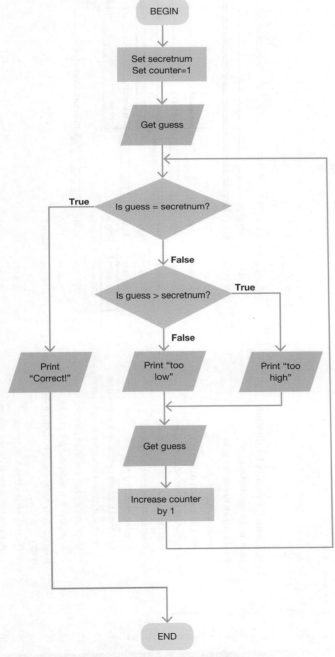

Figure 5.5 Flowchart for the high low game

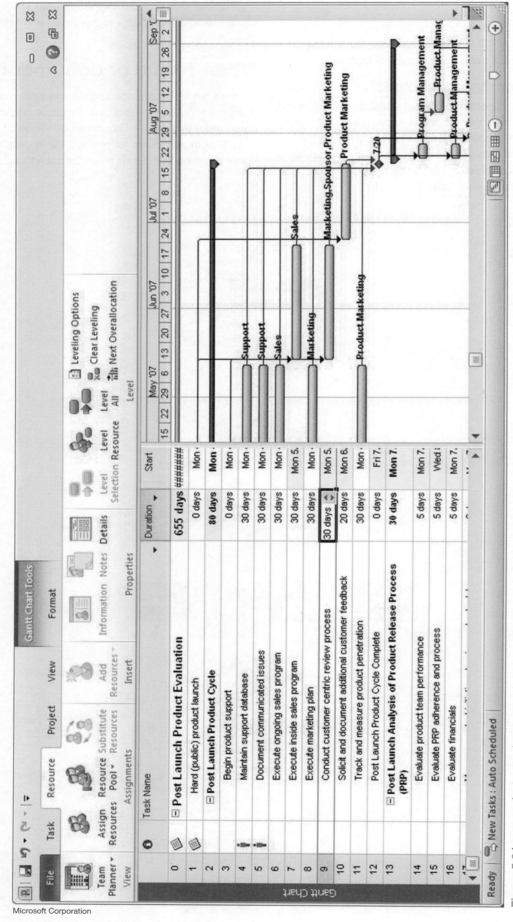

Microsoft Corporation

Figure 5.6 Large projects are documented using professional project management software tools. Here is an example of a Gantt chart.

This class activity is a race to see who can first collect a complete hand of 12 cards arranged so that each word is paired with its matching diagram.

Make a copy of this page for each class member. Cut up all the cards and shuffle them face down. Each person then picks up 12 cards randomly. Class members then move around swapping cards (for which they have duplicates) with one another until they hold a complete set of 12. The first person to get 12 different cards arranged in 6 pairs face up on a table with the correct word matched to its correct diagram calls out and is declared winner.

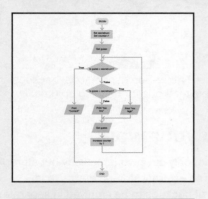

Task	Week 1	Week 2	Week 3
Research ideas			
Create prototype			
Test prototype			
Produce solution			
Evaluate solution			
Documentation			

```
secret = random.randint(1,100)
#print while testing only
print(secret)
#set flag to allow repeated guessing
flag = True
while flag == True:
    guess = input('Your guess?: ')
    #guess is string, so convert to integer
    guess = int(guess)
    # print suitable messages
    if guess < secret:
        print('Too low')
    elif guess > secret:
        print('Too high')
    else:
        print('Correct!')
        #set flag when correct guess
        flag=False
```

Flowchart

Timeline

Commenting

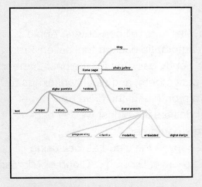

0.9.1
0.9.2
1.0
1.0.5
1.0.6
2.0

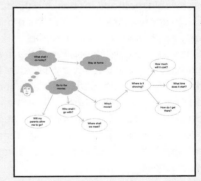

Site map

Versioning

Mind mapping

Figure 5.7

THE IMPORTANCE OF DATA BACKUP

The first time someone takes the importance of backing up seriously is usually the moment they first lose work because they failed to backup! Imagine losing a Higher School Certificate (HSC) major computing project you had worked on all year. This happens to students who do not take the precaution of backing data up seriously.

When computers are working we never imagine that something might happen to them, such as a file becoming corrupted or a hard drive being stolen from our home.

Imagine how critical it is for the Australian Tax Office or for banks to make sure they never lose data. Companies such as Google, Facebook, Apple and Microsoft all have careful backup strategies.

A typical large company with terabytes of data would use distributed servers at multiple locations and have multiple backups. It would use backup data centres in other cities linked by fibre optic cable. These locations are synchronized so a disaster at either location is automatically switched over to the other location. All data is backed up to tape every night at both locations.

Tape is still a common media for nightly backup data. All these systems have uninterrupted power supplies (batteries) with automatic-starting generators that provide backup power within a few minutes.

Backup methods

Grandfather-Father-Son generational backups are one of the most reliable methods for backing up data. There are many possible approaches to this but the most common repeats a weekly cycle, four times in a month.

Once each week (say on Friday), a *full backup* (Father) is made of all data. Each work day after that until the next Friday, daily backups (Son) are made containing only new or changed data from that day. These are called *incremental* backups. The daily Son backups use separate media each day for one week and the next week these are recorded over. Weekly Father backups use separate media each week for four weeks.

Once a month a copy is made of the complete data to a Grandfather backup. There may be more than one of these over a few months.

This process means the business has a weekly 'snapshot' of the complete files as they were at the start of the week, and a record of daily file changes created during the week. Table 5.2 on the following page illustrates this.

Figure 5.8 Grandfather-Father-Son generational backups are one of the most reliable methods for backing up data.

Backing up your work

All students should not only save work regularly but store backup copies using an external storage device. It is important for copies of backups to be archived in separate locations or countries.

Figure 5.9 A typical external removable hard drive used for backups of data.

Backup tools are available for all computers. Apple computers include an automatic backup tool called Time Machine, which saves hourly backups for the past 24 hours, daily backups for the past month, and weekly backups for everything older than a month until the drive runs out of space. At that point, it deletes the oldest weekly backup. It can be used to restore a computer.

Many users store a copy in the cloud as well using services such as Google Drive, Dropbox, iCloud or Microsoft OneDrive.

It is wise also to make regular backups using external hard drives and ask a friend or relative to mind it at another location.

9780170411820

Table 5.2 This Grandfather-Father-Son backup cycle requires 10 separate media

Week	Friday	Monday	Tuesday	Wednesday	Thursday
1	Daily incremental backup (Son 1) Weekly full backup (Father 1)	Daily incremental backup (Son 1)	Daily incremental backup (Son 2)	Daily incremental backup (Son 3)	Daily incremental backup (Son 4)
2	Daily incremental backup (Son 1) Weekly full backup (Father 2)	Daily incremental backup (Son 1)	Daily incremental backup (Son 2)	Daily incremental backup (Son 3)	Daily incremental backup (Son 4)
3	Daily incremental backup (Son 1) Weekly full backup (Father 3)	Daily incremental backup (Son 1)	Daily incremental backup (Son 2)	Daily incremental backup (Son 3)	Daily incremental backup (Son 4)
4	Daily incremental backup (Son 1) Weekly full backup (Father 4) Monthly full backup (Grandfather 1)	Daily incremental backup (Son 1)	Daily incremental backup (Son 2)	Daily incremental backup (Son 3)	Daily incremental backup (Son 4)
Rotate back to start					

Using what you have learnt, complete this record of a backup regime for your own computer using Table 5.3. You will be limited by the number of storage media you have.

Backup media

- Cloud (name: _____)
- External drive 1
- External drive 2
- External drive 3
- Other

Backup software

_____

_____

_____

My monthly backup regime

First briefly describe and then complete the table.

_____

_____

_____

_____

_____

Table 5.3

Week	Friday	Monday	Tuesday	Wednesday	Thursday
1					
2					
3					
4					
Rotate back to start					

Identify

1 What are three broad categories of documentation in project management?

_____

2 Identify five examples of appropriate written documentation for digital projects.

_____

_____

_____

3 Identify five examples of appropriate visual documentation for digital projects.

_____

_____

_____

_____

4 Give an outline for a Grandfather-Father-Son backup process.

_____

_____

Analyse

5 A digital project has the following versioning history. Provide a brief outline of what can be inferred about the versions of the project they represent.

- 0.5.1 _____
- 0.5.2 _____
- 1.0 _____
- 1.0.5 _____
- 1.5 _____
- 2.0 _____

6 Identify and compare two different forms of commenting used by a programmer when writing code and justify their use.

_____

_____

_____

_____

Research

7 Research the backup routines for businesses such as banks where security of data storage is absolutely critical.

_____

_____

_____

06 UNDERSTANDING MOBILE DEVICES AND WIRELESS NETWORKS

OUTCOMES

Australian curriculum content descriptions:
- Investigate how data is transmitted and secured in wired, wireless and mobile networks, and how the specifications affect performance (ACTDIK023) (AC)
- Investigate the role of hardware and software in managing, controlling and securing the movement of and access to data in networked digital systems (ACTDIK034) (AC)

GLOSSARY

bandwidth In computing, bandwidth is the data bit rate and is measured in bits per second. In wireless communication, bandwidth is the frequency range between highest and lowest frequencies and is measured in Hertz

Bluetooth A wireless technology standard for exchanging data over short distances from fixed and mobile devices

cellular network A communication network made up of geographic locations called cells, which each have a cell site or base station providing the network coverage. When a user moves between cells, the transmission will be transferred from cell site to cell site (also known as a mobile network)

LAN (local area network) A network that may comprise wired and/or wireless elements and typically connects devices in a single building or group of buildings within a limited geographical area

WAN (wide area network) A network that may comprise wired and/or wireless elements covering a large geographic area and often involving leased circuits and used to connect separate LANs. The Internet can be considered a WAN

wired network A network in which data is transferred between two or more devices by Ethernet cables

wireless network A network in which data is transferred between two or more devices not connected by an electrical conductor

WiFi A wireless protocol based on the IEEE 802.11 standards used in wireless local area networking (LAN)

WIRELESS NETWORKS

We saw in *Digital Technologies 7 & 8* how **wired networks** operate.

We look now at how **wireless networks** operate. The most common examples of wireless networks we encounter are mobile phone **cellular networks** and **WiFi**. **Bluetooth** is also a wireless connection method, but usually just between two devices close together.

The growth in wireless networks has been huge. There are now 8 billion mobile phones in use around the world.

Wireless signals will only reach a limited distance, so mobile networks depend on carefully positioned towers to hand over the connection as the device moves from one area to another. If the signal can't reach the device, then the connection will drop out.

Figure 6.1 Mobile networks depend on carefully positioned towers to hand over the connection as the device moves from one area to another.

How does a mobile phone system work?

A mobile phone and a mobile phone tower both transmit and receive radio waves. Radio waves form a part of the electromagnetic (EMF) spectrum, of which ordinary visible light is another part.

The phone transmits a very weak signal and the towers transmit strong ones. This is a deliberate design feature as base stations with huge, high-powered antennae can pick up faint signals from many mobiles, otherwise our phones would need massive antennas and giant power supplies and we would no longer be able to call them mobiles!

The strength of the signal from the tower is indicated by 'bars' on your phone. This strength is affected by many things, including the distance between the phone and the nearest tower and the obstacles between them.

To lengthen battery life, a mobile phone is designed to use only the minimum power necessary to communicate with the nearest mobile tower. When your phone has poor connectivity, it boosts the signal and your battery drains faster.

Each connection must operate on a different frequency, so towers sharing overlapping areas use different frequencies.

A simple call

If a phone in one cell calls a second phone in another cell, the call doesn't pass directly between the phones, but from the first phone to the first base station, then to the next base station, and then to the second phone.

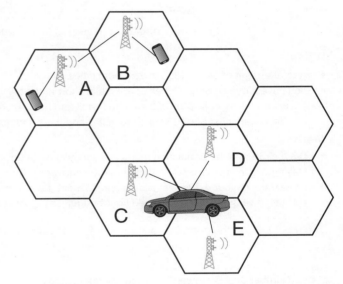

Figure 6.2 Areas served by towers are usually represented by hexagons.

A travelling call

When your phone is moving between cells on a journey, it is constantly sending signals so that the network always knows which tower is closest to your phone.

Activity: Mobile tower simulation

This activity will help you understand the challenges involved in designing wireless networks to cover populations the size of cities such as Sydney and Melbourne.

Follow the weblink from the *Digital Technologies 9 & 10* website to the Australian Bureau of Statistics map showing population densities for Sydney and Melbourne (see Figure 6.3).

Weblink

The task

Imagine you have a limited budget and the job of designing the location of towers to reach the most people.

You can choose whatever combinations of towers you wish, as long as you stay within your budget.

This activity will make you aware of some of the challenges facing the designers of cellular networks.

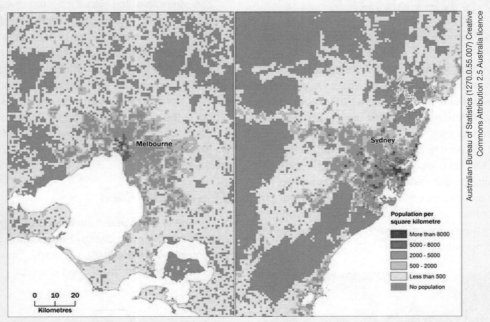

Population per square kilometre

- More than 8000
- 5000 - 8000
- 2000 - 5000
- 500 - 2000
- Less than 500
- No population

Figure 6.3 Population density in Melbourne and Sydney

Rules

- A total budget of $4.5 million covers both cities.
- You have a choice of two types of towers (a short and a tall version).
  - Short towers cost $450 000 each to install and have a radial range of 10 km.
  - Tall towers cost $500 000 each to install and have a radial range of 15 km.

Method

1 Draw circles on the population maps of Sydney and Melbourne to provide the greatest population reach possible while staying within your budget. You may use any draw or paint computer application for this task.
2 Keep track of your expenses using a spreadsheet. Enter formulas in your spreadsheet and decide the combination of short and tall towers that will not exceed your budget. Use goal seeking if you wish.

Table 6.1 Decide the combination of short and tall towers that will not exceed your budget

	A	B	C	D
1	Number of short towers	Number of tall towers	Total cost	Amount over/under budget
2		=450000*A2+500000*B2	=4500000−C2	

3 Open the Melbourne-Sydney density map in a draw software application such as Adobe Illustrator.
4 Using your software, draw circles at the correct radius according to the Rules above, using the scale shown at the bottom left on the map.
5 Duplicate these circles and experiment with various positions to cover as much as possible of the denser population areas and still stay within your budget.
6 Record what you learned about tower placement.

_____

_____

_____

_____

_____

Real-world base stations

Actual mobile cell coverage area is affected by base station output power and environment. A large number of base stations are needed in areas with many high buildings. There are over 3000 base stations in Sydney alone!

A typical base station can handle about 160 voice channels. You can image how impossible mobile communication is when large crowds use their phones at the one time – such as New Year's Eve celebrations. In country areas where there are large open spaces, the base stations will be far apart and the cell reach radius will be around 10–32km.

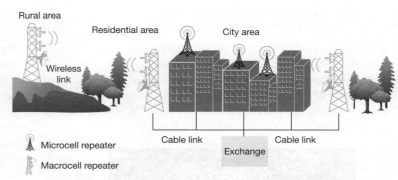

Figure 6.4 Mobile coverage area is affected by base station output power and environmental obstacles

Standard **bandwidths** used by carriers (e.g. Telstra, Vodafone, Optus) in Australia are 10 MHz–20MHz. With the introduction of smartphones, carriers have had to increase the bandwidth and the number of base stations to make sure the Internet does not become slow during peak periods.

Web probe: Mobile base stations near you

1   Use your postcode to find out how many mobile base stations are in your postcode area by using the site search tool at the Radio Frequency National Site Archive website.

2   How many are in your postcode? _____

3   What was the highest number of base stations among postcodes in your class? _____

4   Official data relating to possible health risks associated with mobile base stations are provided by the Australian Radiation Protection and Nuclear Safety Agency. Follow the weblink from the *Digital Technologies 9 & 10* website and summarise their fact sheet relating to this issue.

_____

_____

_____

_____

_____

_____

_____

_____

INFOBIT: WIFI AND BLUETOOTH

Bluetooth is used to connect two devices. Bluetooth technology is used for transferring small amounts of data between two devices around 10 metres apart such as headsets, printers, speakers or even remote controlled robots. Bluetooth does not need a central device such as a router and is easy to set up simply by pairing the devices.

WiFi is used to provide high-speed Internet access to many devices without the need for a wired network. WiFi suits full-scale networks, can connect multiple devices, has a greater range of around 30 metres, better security (if configured properly) and is faster than Bluetooth. Find out what Australia's role was in the development of WiFi.

Figure 6.5 Bluetooth and WiFi are both standards for common wireless communication around the home.

Left to right: Shutterstock.com/Marco Rosales; Shutterstock.com/creative ideas

Web probe: The need for speed

Weblink

In this activity you will compare the speeds of your computer using a wired versus an unwired home or school Internet connection and also your mobile phone using WiFi versus a cellular connection.

1   Select one of the test tools available online. Weblinks provided at the *Digital Technologies 9 & 10* website.

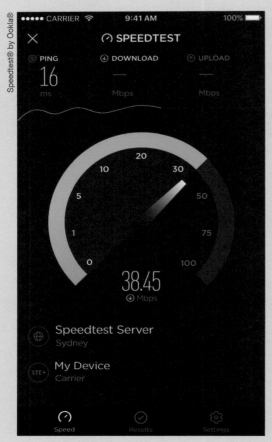

Figure 6.6 The speedtest phone app for testing WiFi and cellular download and upload speeds.

2   Design a spreadsheet similar to Table 6.2. Save it as a template. Include a formula to calculate the average of your results for the averages row.

3   Record your test for each of the four Internet connection scenarios in the table. Repeat the test five times and average the results by using a spreadsheet.

4   Which is faster: WiFi on smartphones or WiFi on computers? Why do you think this is true?

_____

_____

_____

_____

5   Which is faster: WiFi on smartphones or cellular on smartphones? Why do you think this is true?

_____

_____

_____

_____

6   Repeat the experiment using another of our speed test sites. Did one speed test site have consistently higher or lower results? If so, why?

_____

_____

_____

_____

Table 6.2

| Test site | Computer | | Mobile phone | |
	Scenario 1 Laptop/desktop using fixed line (wired) connection	Scenario 2 Laptop/desktop using WiFi (unwired) connection	Scenario 3 Mobile phone using WiFi (unwired) connection	Scenario 4 Mobile phone using cellular (unwired) connection
	Speed in Mbps	Speed in Mbps	Speed in Mbps	Speed in Mbps
Test 1				
Test 2				
Test 3				
Test 4				
Test 5				
Averages				

9780170411820

7 Which website interface of these four speed test tools do you prefer? Why?

_____

_____

_____

_____

_____

_____

8 From the two test tables, select the table with the fastest overall results. Compare your speeds with stated averages for your region/city using the *Australian City listing* tab at Testmy Broadband website.

_____

_____

_____

_____

_____

_____

_____

9 Use the FAQ provided on the speed.io site to summarise the possible causes of slow connections.

_____

_____

_____

_____

_____

_____

_____

_____

Knowledge probe: Wired versus wireless networks

Complete this table comparing wired and wireless networks. Use the Internet to conduct your research.

Knowledge
Probe

Table 6.3

Characteristic	Wired networks	Wireless networks
How hard is it to set up?		
Security		
Cost		
How hard is it to connect a new device?		
How good is it for mobile devices?		

Characteristic	Wired networks	Wireless networks
Reliability		
Speed in mbps and bandwidth		
Strength of signal		
Interference		
Connection set up time		
Standards		

Class activity: Know your network

1 If your school has a technical assistant, invite them to your class to talk about the school's network. Ask them to explain the map of the school network, its switches, routers and other features. (Brainstorm some questions ahead of time to ask.)

2 Write something that you have learnt about the school network.

_____

_____

_____

_____

_____

_____

3 Business networks can be quite complex. Figure 6.7 shows a diagram of a business **LAN (local area network)**. LANs can be connected over large distances, such as between regions or across the globe, to form **WANs (wide area networks)**. The Internet can be considered a WAN.

Sketch a rough diagram of your network on a piece of paper. Simplify it by combining classrooms into larger units. Use icons like those in Figure 6.7, or use symbols instead. Include locations of:
- routers
- switches
- WiFi access points
- servers
- Ethernet cabling
- Ethernet ports
- fibre cabling
- Internet access
- the main distribution board.

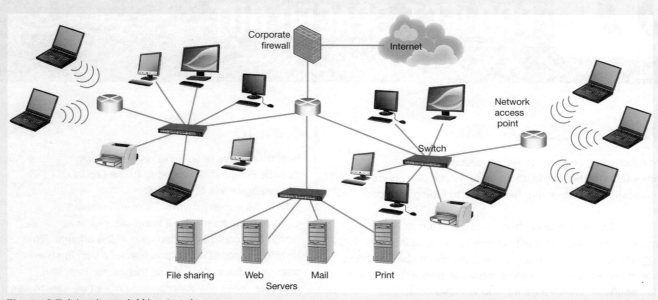

Figure 6.7 A business LAN network

REVIEW

Identify

1 What are the main physical obstacles to mobile wireless communication?

_____

_____

2 What is one difference between Bluetooth and WiFi wireless communication?

_____

Analyse

3 Compare typical wireless and wired networks referring to latency security and interference.

_____

_____

4 Describe the main features of your own school's network.

_____

_____

Research

5 Read the 'Wireless case study' provided as a resource on the _Digital Technologies 9 & 10_ website. Outline the main features of its wireless network and describe a second example of the use of wireless networks for monitoring and controlling a remote site.

_____

_____

_____

PROJECT: SPACED OUT

USING ABSTRACTION

We have learnt that one of the important steps in computational thinking is *abstraction*, where we reduce complexity by capturing a main idea and hiding a lot of detail.

In programming this is often done using *functions* (and *classes* in the case of object-oriented programming). In this programming project we apply the principle of abstraction to English sentences. We create a model sentence (a *template*) and use this to create a game. You will also be able to practise your handling of text strings in your chosen general-purpose programming language.

THE TASK

You have been asked to write a program for children to be known as 'spaced out', which generates funny or crazy stories where blanked out words are replaced by words chosen by the user. For example:

Original version: 'Douglas Engelbart called his invention a mouse because its electrical cord looked like a tail.'

Spaced-out version: '_____ called his _____ a _____ because its _____ looked like a ___.'

Example of a final version: '*Bart Simpson* called his *bed* a *clothes dryer* because its *lid* looked like a *spaceship*.'

Lewis Carroll used this idea for a poem by the Mad Hatter in his book *Alice's Adventures in Wonderland*:

TWINKLE, TWINKLE, little bat!

How I wonder what you're at!

Up above the world you fly,

Like a tea-tray in the sky.

Lewis Carroll

Figure 7.1

Defining

Weblink

1 First try out this online version of a similar activity. Follow the weblink from the *Digital Technologies 9 & 10* website.

2 Taking the nursery rhyme 'Twinkle, Twinkle Little Star' as a prototype template, highlight words that could be substituted in the original. Now rewrite the poem with blank spaces replacing the changed words. We will use this as our template, however, users of your program will not be able to see it.

_____

_____

_____

_____

_____

_____

_____

_____

3 What instructions would you give someone for choosing random words, so a computer program could generate a crazy version that still rhymes, as the original does? (example: 'Choose noun 1' then 'Choose a verb that rhymes with noun 1'…)?

_____

_____

_____

_____

_____

_____

_____

_____

Designing

1 Write an algorithm using structured English that takes users' input and inserts each word at correct places in your template.
2 Explain how the computational principle of abstraction was used to develop this game.

_____

_____

_____

_____

_____

_____

Implementing

1 Write code to implement your algorithm.
2 Develop a second template that inserts the same words but uses a random function to select between the two templates.
3 If your programming language's integrated development environment (IDE) allows you to output using different fonts (for example, ActionScript if using Adobe Animate), use this feature to output your poem, inspired by Figure 7.1.
4 If you need help, a simple example written in Python 3 is provided as a resource on the _Digital Technologies 9 & 10_ website.

Evaluating

1 Have others test your program and suggest improvements.
2 What did you learn from this project?

_____

_____

_____

_____

_____

_____

_____

3 Identify improvements or additional features you could include.

_____

_____

_____

_____

_____

_____

_____

_____

_____

EXTENSION

Develop a second program that uses a longer story template similar to the online game you explored in Defining. Record your notes below.

_____

_____

_____

_____

_____

_____

_____

_____

_____

_____

_____

_____

_____

$$6 > 3 > 10 > 5 > 16 > 8 > 4 > 2 > 1$$

Figure 8.1

Hailstone numbers are also known as odds and evens chains, or wondrous numbers. They are produced using these very simple rules:

- Take any positive integer (number).
- If a number is **even**, divide it by 2.
- If a number is **odd**, multiply it by 3 and add 1.
- This continues until you arrive at 1.

Here is an example starting with six:

6 > 3 > 10 > 5 > 16 > 8 > 4 > 2 > 1

Notice this chain is nine numbers long.

Here is another example starting with 13:

13 > 40 > 20 > 10 > 5 > 16 > 8 > 4 > 2 > 1

Notice this chain is 10 steps long.

We will try to answer two questions:

- Will chains always end up at 1?
- What integer has the longest chain if we start in the range 1 to 100?

Activity: Hailstone numbers

Explain why these numbers are called hailstone numbers.

_____

_____

_____

_____

_____

_____

_____

_____

THE TASK

Your project is to design, code and test a program that can calculate the odds and evens rule so that a Year 7 maths teacher can use it with Year 7 classes to help answer the two questions above.

Your program must be able to find the integer that produces the longest chain when an upper range is chosen. You will be helped here developing an early version of your code. Then you will work on your own to improve the program and add features.

REMEMBER THE RULES

If number is **even**: then $\div 2$
If number is **odd**: then $\times 3 + 1$
Stop at 1!

INFOBIT: THE COLLATZ CONJECTURE

Hailstone numbers form one of the great unanswered and unproven problems in mathematics. It is known as the Collatz conjecture. A conjecture is like an opinion or a proposal. The Collatz conjecture centres around this question:

Does every positive integer always reach 1 if the hailstone rule is applied?

The conjecture states that the answer is yes, but no one has ever been able to prove this! If the answer is no, it must be because there is some starting number that produces a sequence that does not contain 1. This might be because it creates a repeating cycle that excludes 1, or always gets larger. No such sequence has ever been found.

9780170411820

Defining

1 Using an Internet search, find the integer less than 1 million with the most steps.

_____

_____

2 How many steps did it take to reach 1?

_____

_____

3 Research online to find what most mathematicians think is the answer to the Collatz conjecture.

_____

_____

_____

4 First understand the problem by trying out integers by hand from 1 to 15 using Table 8.1. As you complete it, can you see a way to use shortcuts?

The longest chain is 20 steps. Which integer was this?

_____

Table 8.1

Integer	Chain	Length
1	1	1
2	2 > 1	2
3		
4		
5		
6	6 > 3 > 10 > 5 > 16 > 8 > 4 > 2 > 1	9
7		
8		
9		
10		
11		
12		
13		
14		
15		

Designing

Our first problem is to find an algorithm to test if a number is even or odd.

There are a number of ways to do this. When we divide an integer by 2 we get a whole number only if it is even. Can we use this in our algorithm?

All computer languages have a function to find remainders after division.

In Python it is called the *modulo* operator, and its symbol is %. Find out what it is in the coding language you use in class.

Here are some examples:

```
7 % 3 = 1
17 % 3 = 2
123 % 25 = 23
6 % 2 = 0
```

Can you see how this works?
Using algebraic language:

```
x % y gives the remainder after
division of x by y.
```

1   Test this function using the above examples as well as some of your own.

```
>>> 123 % 25
23
>>> 12 % 2
0
```

2   Test a few even integers to see what happens when you make the second number '2'.
3   Test a few odd integers to see what happens when you make the second number '2'.
4   Did you find that even integers always give '0'?

_____

5   Explain why this is true.

_____

_____

_____

_____

6   How can we use this as part of a selection algorithm to code our hailstone numbers program?

_____

_____

_____

_____

_____

_____

_____

The basic program: Version 1.0

Here is a first step in structured English. Examine it carefully to understand how it works. Keep track of your versions by using version numbering, which is explained in Chapter 5. This is a good habit to get into as a coder! It also ensures you do not lose older versions as you change your code.

Working versions written in Python 3.0 are available online on the *Digital Technologies 9 & 10* website but try coding yourself without looking at these.

```
BEGIN
   select an integer x
   display x followed by '>' symbol
   IF x % 2 equals 0 THEN
      divide x by 2
   ELSE
      multiply x by 3 and add 1
   END IF
   x becomes new value
   display new value of x followed by
      '>' symbol
END
```

Implementing

1   Now translate your structured English to code in your chosen computer language. Remember to add comments explaining your code.
2   A problem is that this version only steps through once. Modify this with a while loop to make it repeat until x becomes 1. Try to print the chain on the same line. Note that in Python 3 if you want printing to remain on the same line with a '>' printed between values, add a comma followed by end = '>'

```
print(x,end='>')
```

Adding a counter: Version 2.0

3   Next we want the length of our chain to be printed. We have to add a counter.

Here is the structured English for the code with the steps repeated until the value reaches 1. The length of the chain is printed.

```
BEGIN
   select an integer x
   display x followed by '>' symbol
   set counter to 1
   WHILE x does not equal 1 THEN
      IF x%2 equals 0 THEN
         divide x by 2
      ELSE
         multiply x by 3 and add 1
      END IF
      assign new value to x
      display new value of x + '>'
      increment counter by 1
   END WHILE
   print counter to give chain length
END
```

9780170411820

Genuine computing power! Version 3.0

4 Remember how long it took you to complete the chains for all integers 1 to 15 by hand? Now you have the earlier versions working, your task is to modify your program to allow a user to enter an integer and for the program to calculate all the chains beginning at 1 and up to and including that value.

Entering 15 should thus produce all chains from 1 to 15.

Improve printing times: Version 3.1

Printing to screen on each calculation takes a long time, even for a computer!

5 Modify your code to include a variable to remember the string until the chain has finished calculations, then print it. Use something like this:

```
chain = chain + x + '>'
```

This is known as concatenation. Look up the meaning of this computing term, which is commonly used in string operations such as this. Don't forget to reinitialise it to an empty string each time.

Use even more computing power: Version 4.0

6 Your final challenge is to add a feature to report the integer with the longest chain within the range the user requested. You will need something like this:

```
set longest_chain to 1
if current_chain > longest_chain:
    set longestchain to current_chain
    set integer_with_longest_chain to
        current integer
```

Evaluating

1 Test your program and have others test it and suggest improvements.

2 Use first version 4 then version 3 of your program to find the numbers with the two longest chains for integers 1 to 100. Write down the answer and explain the great difference in time taken.

_____

_____

_____

3 What is the chain length for the integer 837799?

_____

4 Have you proven that all integers will reach 1?

_____

_____

5 Search the Internet for the Collatz sequence. Record what you learn.

_____

_____

_____

_____

_____

6 What did you learn from this project?

_____

_____

_____

_____

_____

7 Identify additional features you could include.

_____

_____

_____

_____

A FURTHER CHALLENGE

Some additional challenges:
- offer users the choice of setting both lower and upper limits, rather than always having to start at 1.
- Hailstone numbers can be implemented using a spreadsheet. See if you can do this.

Learning to code

If you have read Chapter 3 in _Digital Technologies 7 & 8_ and have completed the programming projects in both books then you have gained lots of experience in visual, general-purpose and object-oriented programming. However, perhaps you wish to develop your coding skills further, experience programming languages other than ones used in class or just explore? There are many free or low-cost options available. Here are some suggestions for great places to start (weblinks are provided at the _Digital Technologies 9 & 10_ website):

- Code.org
- Grok Learning
- Khan Academy
- Codecademy
- Udemy
- W3schools.com
- Swift Playgrounds (iPad)

Weblink

09 PROJECT: PROGRAMMING AN ANIMATED GAME

THE TASK

We will use Adobe Animate to program the 'Hi-Lo' game using animations as user feedback.

The completed animation *rocket_launch_animation.fla* necessary for this project is provided on the *Digital Technologies 9 & 10* website. If you wish to create this animation from scratch yourself, you can do so. We provide a bonus project 'Create your rocket launch animation' on the website to guide you.

Defining

1   In the Hi-Lo game users have to guess a number between 1 and 100. We will create three animations:
   - If their guess is too high, the user will see an animation of a rocket that overshoots a planet.
   - If their guess is too low, the user will see an animation of a rocket that undershoots a planet.
   - If their guess is correct, the user will see an animation of a rocket landing on a planet.
2   We will control the game by writing a simple program in Animate's own scripting language called ActionScript 3.0. This language is similar to JavaScript.
3   Write down at least five criteria for evaluating if your project is successful once complete.

_____

_____

_____

_____

_____

_____

_____

_____

_____

_____

_____

_____

_____

Designing

1   Draw a flowchart for the program logic. Refer to *Digital Technologies 7 & 8* Chapter 3 if you are unsure.
2   Design a user interface for your project on paper. Here is an example:

Rocket must land on planet

Rocket and gantry   User interface for guesses   Launch button   User feedback. Here we have made the secret number visible to assist in debugging.

Figure 9.1 A possible interface design: text boxes for user input, feedback messages for users, space for the animations to play and a button to launch the rocket. A debugging feature can also be seen.

We will have three versions of our rocket animation.
- The animation for guesses that are too low will show the rocket undershooting the planet. This will begin at frame 50.
- The animation for guesses that are too high will show the rocket overshooting the planet. This will begin at frame 200.
- The animation for guesses that are correct will show the rocket landing on the planet. This will begin at frame 350.

Adobe Animate provides snippets of codes that will make programming easier.

Our game works like this:
- Frame 1 will be used to define variables. As the playhead enters frame 1, the ActionScript code in this frame will set up the secret number and set the counter to 0.
- Playhead stops on frame 2 and waits for player to make a guess and press a button. The correct rocket animation will play with feedback to the player on number of guesses and whether high, low or correct.
- After each animation plays, the playhead returns to frame 2.

Implementing

Setting up layers

1 Open a new Animate project: File > New (Set Type to ActionScript 3).

2 Open the completed animation *rocket_launch_animation.fla* provided online. Carefully select all the layers and all their frames from this animation (rocket animation, planet, stars, gantry, audio, etc.). Right-click and select Copy Layers (not normal Copy and Paste!).

3 Create a layer in your new Animate document and right-click to Paste Layers into this document.

4 Duplicate twice this rocket animation layer (thus creating three versions). Rename these 'lo_anim', 'hi_anim' and 'landing_anim'.

5 We need to make sure the background, stars and planets are visible throughout the game so extend the timelines of all layers to reach frame 450.

6 The three duplicated rocket motion tweened animations must be positioned as follows:
   - On the new *lo_anim* layer carefully select all frames of the 100 frame animation of the rocket and drag these to commence at frame 50.
   - On the new *hi_anim* layer, carefully select all frames of the 100 frame animation of the rocket and drag these to commence at frame 200.
   - On the new *landing_anim* layer, carefully select all frames of the 100 frame animation of the rocket and drag these to commence at frame 350.

   Control > Test and let the main timeline play to the end. The three animations should play in sequence and the background and planet should be visible throughout. However, all animations are identical at this stage!

7 Adjust the last frame (frame 150) of the lo_anim motion tween so the rocket undershoots the planet (see Figure 9.2).

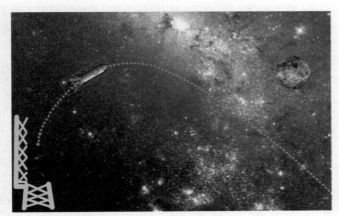

Figure 9.2

8 Adjust the last frame of the hi_anim motion tween (frame 300) so the rocket overshoots the planet (see Figure 9.3).

Figure 9.3

9 Adjust the last frame of the landing_anim motion tween (frame 450) to make sure the rocket lands on the planet (see Figure 9.4).

Figure 9.4

10 Control > Test. and let the main timeline play to the end. The three animations should now each be different: first undershooting, then overshooting, then landing.
   We have reserved frame 1 for game setup.
   This frame will only be seen once as during the game we will make the playhead return to frame 2. If we did not do this, a new secret number would be created each turn – making it very hard to guess!

Setting up textboxes and a button in frame 2

We create a text box in which the user will enter their guess (known as an *input text box*) and another to contain our feedback messages (known as a *dynamic text box*). A third type is known as static text and is used for text that does not change.

11 Name a new layer 'messages'. Create a blank keyframe in frame 2 and use the Text tool to draw a text box in which messages will appear.

12 Select the Properties panel, name this field 'message_box' and set it to dynamic text using the drop-down menu. Set Font Style and Size and in the Properties box click the button to embed the font you are using. It can be tricky to make this visible. To do so there is a box that must be selected in the Properties panel. It is shown highlighted in Figure 9.5.

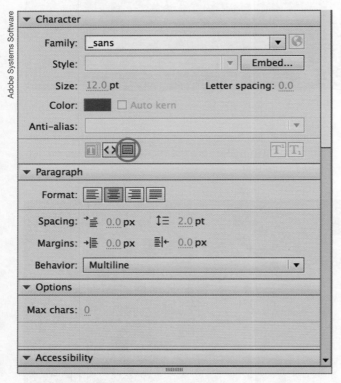

Figure 9.5 Select this button at the bottom of the Character section to make textbox visible

13 Name a new layer 'guesses'. Create a blank keyframe in frame 2 and use the Text tool to draw a text box in which guesses will appear. Select the Properties panel, name this field 'guess_box' and set it to Input text using the drop-down menu. Set Font Style and Size and in the Properties box click the button to embed the font you are using. Give it a visible background as in previous step (result is shown in Figure 9.6).

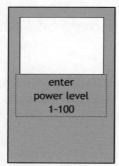

Figure 9.6 Creating a message panel in the guesses layer

Create a button in frame 2

14 Create a new layer 'button' and in frame 2 draw a circle (see Figure 9.7).

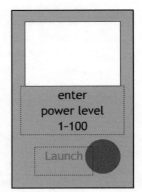

Figure 9.7 The message panel now with button added

15 To turn this into a button, double-click to select the whole circle then choose Modify > Convert to Symbol, give the symbol a name and select Button from the drop-down menu. Double-click on this new button symbol. You will see a layer appear in the timeline with Up, Over, Down and Hit. These allow the user to receive visual feedback when the mouse is over or presses the button. Add a keyframe for Over and as feedback change the fill colour for the button. You could also shift it slightly to the right. Do the same for Down (see Figure 9.8).

16 Select the new button in the main timeline and in Properties give it the Instance name 'play_button'. Note that this is an instance of the button object you created and stored in the library. Do not give button objects and their instances the same name. It is good habit to name instances consistently using a convention such as: 'somename_button'.

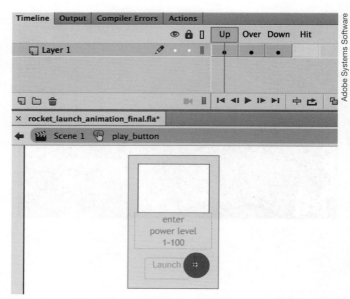

Figure 9.8 Creating a button symbol with user feedback for mouse over and down

9780170411820

Set up Actions layer

All our programming code will be placed in a layer in the main timeline we will call Actions. Create this layer and name it 'Actions'.

We need to declare integer variables for both the secret number and for the player's guess.

We also need to declare a string variable for the result each time ('too high', 'too low' or 'correct').

1   Move to Frame 1 of the Actions layer. Make sure there is a keyframe there. Click the Actions tab alongside the Timeline tab. Type this into the code editor:

```
var secret, counter, guess:int;
var result:String;
```

2   We now need the playhead to stop at frame 2 and wait for a player to guess a number. Create a keyframe in the Actions layer at frame 2 and type this into the code editor:

```
stop();
```

Observe the small letter 'a' for Actions appearing in frames that contain code scripts.

Making the playhead return to frame 2 each turn

In the Actions layer, move to each frame where each of the three animations end. At each of these create a keyframe in the Actions layer and using the Action code tab to bring up the code editor and type the following in the empty code editor:

```
gotoAndPlay(2);
```

In this way you have created code that is only read when the playhead arrives at that frame. The playhead then returns to frame 2, stops and waits for a button press, as we placed the `stop()` instruction in our code at frame 2. The listener code associated with our launch button will override the stop commands in a script.

Generating a random integer 1–100

The built-in maths function `Math.random()` generates random decimal values less than 1. Multiplying by 100 gives a random decimal number less than 100. We then need to use `int()` with this result to convert the decimal to an integer.

```
int(Math.random()*100)
```

However, this will only give us values 0 to 99. To fix this we can add 1:

```
int(Math.random()*100)+1
```

Finally, we will need to initialise our counter and prepare a beginning message for the player. We will add the secret random number to show it temporarily while we are debugging.

Add these additional lines to your Actions layer frame 1 code and it should now look like this:

```
var secret, counter, guess:int;
var result:String;

secret = int(Math.random()*100) + 1;
counter = 0
result = "Find the correct power
    level 1-100 to land the rocket
    on the planet"+secret;
```

Remaining code in frame 2 of the Actions layer

3   We add the message box text field with the value of `result` (which we set up in our code in frame 1) to frame 2. It will now look like this:

```
message_box.text = result;
stop();
```

Don't forget the semi-colons at the end of each line of code!

4   The next step seems unexpected. Event-driven programs with buttons such as ours must watch continuously in case they are pressed. There is a built-in 'event listener' that performs this task. It listens for a press on the `play_button` button and if it detects one this instruction will then run the function, named here as `hi_lo_function`. Add the following code in Frame 2:

```
play_button.addEventListener
    (MouseEvent.CLICK, hi_lo_
    function);

function hi_lo_function
    (event:MouseEvent):void {
    //code for hi_lo_function will go
        here
}
```

The game engine

We now write the main part of the code, again in Frame 2. We provide the start but you need to follow the pattern to work out the rest. If you get stuck you can check a working version online at the *Digital Technologies 9 & 10* website.

5   Complete the code for the hi-lo function. 'void' just means that a value is not being returned by the function. Instead it is performing an action. We need to turn the text typed by the player in `guess_box` into an integer so we can check it mathematically against our secret random value.

```
function hi_lo_function(event:
    MouseEvent): void {
    guess = int(guess_box.text);
    counter = counter + 1;
```

6 The next part of our function will deal with a guess that is too low. We provide you now with an outline of the Frame 2 code. It is your task to fill in the missing parts of the function, shown in red.

```
message_box.text=result;
stop();

play_button.addEventListener
    (MouseEvent.CLICK, hi_lo_function);

function hi_lo_function(event:
  MouseEvent): void {
  guess = int(guess_box.text);
  counter = counter + 1;
  if (fill in this) {
    result = "You undershot the
      planet. Launch attempts:"+
      counter;
    gotoAndPlay(50);

  } else if (fill in this) {
    fill in this;
    fill in this;

  } else if (guess == secret) {
    fill in this;
    fill in this;
  }
}
```

A completed version of this interactive animation is provided on the *Digital Technologies 9 & 10* website titled *rocket_programming_final.fla*.

A note on debugging

Debugging should be ongoing throughout the implementation stage of any project. Check your code regularly. It is far easier to locate an error soon after it occurs than later on! Use this checklist:

- Are you saving ALL versions and not just overwriting each one?
- Have you checked all lines end with semi-colons?
- Have you checked your code carefully for small omissions?
- Do the frame numbers in your code correspond to start and end frames of animations?
- Do the names of your functions match the name inside addEventListener commands?
- Are instances named correctly for each object? It is very easy to name symbols and forget to name instances!

Versions for use on other platforms

Now you have done all the hard work, Animate allows you to create many different versions for delivery of your final product.

Standalone projectors

Projectors are Animate files that bundle your .swf file with the Adobe Flash (the previous name for Animate) Player. Projectors play exactly like a normal application, without the need for a web browser, Flash Player plug-in, Adobe AIR, or any other platform runtimes. When exported, Projector files are generated as standalone .exe files for Windows and a standalone app for Mac.

Choose File > Publish settings … and select the versions you wish to create. Set the path first using the small folder icon.

Note: To create projectors, you need to turn off anti-aliasing for each font. If you get a warning, select your text blocks and set the anti-alias types to Use Device Fonts from the drop-down menu in Character properties.

A number of versions of this project are supplied on the *Digital Technologies 9 & 10* website.

HTML5

Animate lets you publish HTML5 Canvas documents using open web standards. This means your project can be used on any modern browser, including mobile devices. However, you must start with the HTML setting and provide all associated assets.

Evaluating

1 Have another student critically evaluate your project against your criteria chosen under 'Defining', as well as make other suggestions for improvement. This might be hard to hear, but it is essential in real-life projects where reputation, money and time are involved. Record their observations here.

_____

_____

_____

_____

_____

_____

_____

9780170411820

2 Evaluating is also about identifying innovative ways solutions could be used. Can you think of a real-world application that could provide the basic ideas of this project?

_____

_____

_____

_____

_____

_____

3 How could the user interface (UI) for this game be adapted to a virtual reality (VR) environment?

_____

_____

_____

_____

_____

_____

4 Would the user interface layout need to change if this program was adapted for a mobile phone?

_____

_____

_____

_____

_____

5 What did you learn from this project?

_____

_____

_____

_____

_____

6 What would you do differently if you did this again?

_____

_____

_____

_____

_____

_____

_____

7 Identify additional features you could include.

_____

_____

_____

_____

_____

_____

8 Which skills have you learnt that could be transferred to other projects?

_____

_____

_____

_____

_____

_____

_____

FURTHER CHALLENGES

1 Create two additional animations and handle guesses across five ranges rather than three.
2 **Advanced:** Create a different type of interaction where the user must type the launch angle of a rocket object to land on a planet object (as in the game *Angry Birds*).

10 PROJECT: PROGRAMMING AN OBJECT-ORIENTED GAME

THE TASK

In this project you will first learn about **object-oriented programming (OOP)**, then create a text-based role-playing game (RPG) using a guided approach. Finally, you will make the game your own by modifying it and adding features you design yourself.

Overview

This project is in two parts.

1. Knowledge probe: What is OOP?
    You will play the well-known game *Tetris* as an introduction to the concepts involved in OOP.
2. Project: Building an OOP program.
    You will get started with OOP code by creating a working game that you then work on as your project.

    Python 3.0 will be used to demonstrate OOP ideas and for code examples; however, the principles can be adapted to all OOP languages.

Knowledge probe: What is OOP?

The OOP programming approach groups objects that have common characteristics into **classes** with **attributes** and behaviours called **methods**. The analogy of a car company that produces different models is often used to explain OOP principles and its advantages:

Knowledge Probe

Each car model (for example, a hatchback) is considered a separate class described by the factory's blueprints created before any cars exist. This class will have certain properties or attributes such as colour, hatchback door, aircon (yes or no), chassis type, luxury additions (yes or no) and so on. It will also have certain behaviours or methods

such as a speed calculation, fuel usage, cruise control, hatchback opening switch and many more.

When the first hatchback is made it is said to be an **instance** of the hatchback class. Every new hatchback shares the properties and behaviours of the hatchback class. There will be other classes, such as a ute, with its own properties and behaviours.

In fact, we could create a kind of 'super class' called 'car' to which all these subclasses belong and assign to it all the properties and behaviours that all car models possess to save us re-entering them every time a new model is designed.

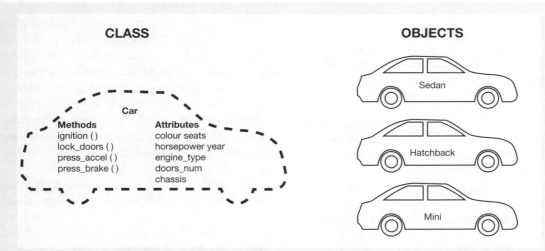

CLASS

Car

Methods
ignition ()
lock_doors ()
press_accel ()
press_brake ()

Attributes
colour seats
horsepower year
engine_type
doors_num
chassis

OBJECTS

Sedan

Hatchback

Mini

Figure 10.1 Using OOP, each model designed by a car company could be considered a separate subclass of the class 'cars'. These subclasses describe the factory's designs created before any cars exist. In OOP, instances are the actual cars after being built. Each physical car is an instance of a particular subclass model and has a colour, seats and engines of particular types.

Why OOP?

Most people first learn to code using procedural methods. You may wonder what the advantages of OOP are. In procedural programming, functions are scattered throughout the code. We will describe two main advantages here.

First, instead of having lots of different functions scattered through a program, making it possible for programmers to lose track of them, OOP collects these and groups them in classes. Second, any data that relates to an object is bundled inside its class. This is important as it can be reused and protected from alteration.

OOP takes functions a step further using a principle called *encapsulation* (think: '*putting things together in a capsule*') by creating classes of related data with methods for accessing and managing that data.

Because OOP is a different way of thinking, it takes time to get used to thinking that way. Instead of first breaking a problem down into lots of functions, we try to identify similar objects and their characteristics.

Skill builder: OOP concepts

Alamy Stock Photo/kern bridges

Figure 10.2 *Tetris* played on a smartphone

1 Go online and play the classic game of *Tetris*.
2 After playing *Tetris* for a while, complete the following table.

Skill builder

Weblink

Table 10.1

Objects	Properties or attributes	Methods or behaviours	Instances
Playing board			
Playing piece			
High-score gallery			
Up next			
On hold			

Although there are seven different block shapes in *Tetris*, they all share the same behaviour. We could say they belong to the same class, which we could call *block*.

Also, although they differ in shape and colour, they all have a colour and a shape. Different blocks are called instances of the *block* class. Each block has at least three *attributes*: orientation, shape and colour. Each block has three *methods*: it can move horizontally, vertically and be rotated.

The playing board could be considered a second class, which we might call *board*. Then we could create other board shapes as instances of this class if we wished.

What does OOP code look like?

Classes

To define a class in Python, we just use the word 'class', followed by the name of the new class. We use a colon after the name but do not use any parentheses. All code after that in the class is indented:

```
class Car:
  more code
  more code
  ...
```

Attributes and methods

We now have a class but it doesn't do anything! If we add variables and a method, we have begun to define our car class (see Figure 10.3.).

Instances

If we now write:

```
sedan=Car()
```

We have created our first car object – a sedan. We say in OOP we have created an *instance* of our car *class*.

It inherits all the characteristics of the car class. Notice the word `self` in our class definition? When Python calls a method, it passes the current object (in this case, sedan) to the method as its first argument. We always have to include the word `self` first in any list of arguments for a method in a class. Otherwise we will get an error because when Python tries to pass in our instance of a car, a sedan, the method would not accept it – it would think it does not accept arguments.

It would be the same if you tried to pass an argument to an ordinary function that had no passing parameters defined.

We use dot notation to call methods belonging to a class and in this case we will call the `moving` method. If we now ran this code:

```
sedan.moving()
```

the output would be:

```
>>>
Varooom!
>>>
```

Now a hatchback has five doors rather than the standard four we built into our car class. How can we change this number for a hatchback?

We cannot access the `number_of_doors` variable inside the class as it is local to the class. This means the variable can only be seen by code inside the class. To solve this we can write a new method `door_count`:

```
def door_count(self):
  print('I have' + str(self.number_
    doors) + 'doors')
```

First we create a hatchback as an instance of the car class:

```
hatchback=car()
```

Now we can change the number of doors for our hatchback instance by writing:

```
hatchback.number_doors = 5
```

Here is our complete code:

```
class Car:
  number_doors=4
  def moving(self):
    print('Varooom!')
  def door_count(self):
    print('I have' + str(self.number_
      doors) + 'doors')
```

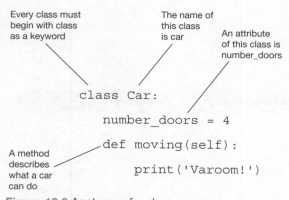

Every class must begin with class as a keyword

The name of this class is car

An attribute of this class is number_doors

A method describes what a car can do

```
class Car:

  number_doors = 4

  def moving(self):

    print('Varoom!')
```

Figure 10.3 Anatomy of a class

9780170411820

Having written the above class definition for `car`, what will be the output of the following?

```
hatchback=Car()
hatchback.moving()
hatchback.number_doors = 5
hatchback.door_count()
```

_____

_____

_____

What will be the output of the following?

```
sedan=Car()
sedan.door_count()
hatchback.door_count()
```

_____

_____

_____

We can also create subclasses. Here we create a subclass of our car class just for four wheel drives so we can add special features. Add the following to the existing code:

```
class FourWD(car):
  def features(self):
    print('I can drive on sand')

beachbeast = FourWD()
```
What output will each of the following produce?

```
beachbeast.features()
```

_____

_____

_____

```
beachbeast.door_count()
```

_____

_____

_____

```
beachbeast.moving()
```

_____

_____

_____

_____

GUIDED PROJECT: BUILDING AN OOP PROGRAM

If you were asked to create a RPG at this stage of your programming experience you would most likely design it by using variables and functions to set up your enemies and a player. OOP offers a better approach.

Understanding classes

Before we start coding our game, we will examine what actual code for a class looks like using Python. Since both monsters and heroes share features, we will bundle everything into one class and call it `LivingThing()`. Every time we want to create either a hero or a monster we could just use this class as its 'rubber stamp' and assign unique attributes to the copy we make.

In Python this might look like this:

```
class LivingThing():
  def __init__(self):
    self.name = 'some name'
    self.health = 1
```

We will examine this code now carefully. We start the class definition with the `class` keyword, followed by the class name and a colon. After this we defined a function, which in classes is called a _method_. This first one looks a bit strange:

```
def __init__(self):
```

`def` here is short for define. This means what follows is a _definition_ of something.

`__init__( )` is a special method called a _constructor_. Constructors are like blueprints for objects – not the objects themselves. When we 'call' a class, a new empty one is created, and the `__init__` method is immediately executed. Its purpose is to create a new object using a pattern we provide. All LivingThings receive its attributes.

We define two attributes: `name` and `health`. These all begin with `self` to show they are member variables belonging to our instances and not just local variables, which disappear after a class is used. Their values can be changed later in the program.

By writing the following we create an _instance_ or copy of a new living thing, in this case our player, using the `LivingThing` as the pattern or rubber stamp.

```
player=LivingThing()
```

We can now do the same to create other creatures. We have seriously reduced the amount of code we need to write by using the same class for both hero and all enemies. We could easily create more `LivingThing` objects, such as enemies:

```
enemy1=LivingThing()
enemy2=LivingThing()
```

Benefits of using classes

Here's where we begin to see another very big benefit of OOP. If another programmer is reading the code, they know they can just look for the class `LivingThing` and find out everything they need to know about `LivingThing`.

Further, they know if they update the `LivingThing` object then all objects created from it will now gain that new feature. This is much easier than trawling through a long procedural program trying to find what parts need to be changed.

Start here: Building the game

Now we understand the concept of a class and its usefulness, we will build a role-playing game. We will first create a bare-bones RPG then build the complete game. Note that you must type code out rather than copying and pasting. In fact, code that is pasted will usually fail to run as it will contain unwanted hidden characters and incorrect indenting and spacing. A critical part of learning to code involves learning the importance of precision. In addition, it will help you learn the ideas far better.

Common issues students face while coding in Python:
- indentation must be correct
- lines with conditionals (if, else, elif, while) and def must be terminated with colons
- quote marks must be correct around strings
- capital letters are important
- opening parentheses and braces must be matched with closing ones.

The approach we will take is to create two subclasses for player and enemies (Monsters) using a `LivingThing` class as the base class for both of these, then set up the attributes and starting values for each.

Create the classes

The player also has a `status class` variable, to be used in battles with monsters. Notice that the monster class is passed two variables (`name` and `health`) when its instances are first created.

Type this:

```
class LivingThing():
  def __init__(self):
    self.name = 'some name'
    self.health = 1
```

```
class Player(LivingThing):
  def __init__(self, name):
    self.name=name
    self.health = 15
    self.status='regular'
```

```
class Monster(LivingThing):
  def __init__(self,name,health):
    self.name=name
    self.health = health
```

Defining the methods

Living things get tired, get hurt and get healed! So we need to create these three methods for our LivingThing class. Any object we then create using this class will be able to get tired, get hurt and be healed.

Type the following inside your LivingThing class after the existing code:

```
def tire(self):
  self.health = self.health - 2
```

```
def hurt(self):
  self.health = self.health - randint
    (0, self.health)
```

```
def heal(self):
  self.health = self.health + 1
```

Describe what each one of these methods does.

_____

_____

_____

_____

Next we need methods for our Player class. We create a method for each of the actions our player needs to perform. At this stage, we will leave these empty by typing the word 'pass' in place of content.

Add these additional methods inside the Player class:

```
def help(self,monster):
  pass
def stats(self,monster):
  pass
def explore(self,monster):
  pass
def run(self,monster):
  pass
def fight(self,monster):
  pass
```

9780170411820

Create command dictionary

We need the player to use simple commands to play the game. These need to run the methods we have now started to write. We will set these up in the form of a Python dictionary data structure where a simple keyword (such as 'help' or 'stats') will send the program to the appropriate method.

Type this at the end of your current code:

```
Commands = {
'help': Player.help,
'stats': Player.stats,
'explore': Player.explore,
'run': Player.run,
'fight': Player.fight
}
```

Create instances

We are ready to create instances. One will be our hero and two will be monsters. First our hero is born as an instance of the subclass player, which belongs to the `LivingThing` main ('super') class. Type this after your class definitions on a new line:

```
name = input('What is your name?  ')
hero = Player(name)
```

To handle multiple monsters we use Pythons' list data structure, sending the monster subclass the two variables it expects, then adding them to a list we call `monsters`:

Type this:

```
goblin=Monster('Goblin',20)
dragon=Monster('Dragon',10)
monsters = []
monsters.append(goblin)
monsters.append(dragon)
```

As each game begins we will randomly choose one of the monsters as our enemy. We will do this by using a very convenient keyword (`choice`) available in Python, which returns a random choice from a list.

Type:

```
monster = choice(monsters)
```

You will need to add the following line as the first line right at the start program in order to import the random module into Python to allow this choice function to work.

```
from random import randint, choice
```

The game

Now we are ready to drive the game. First we deliver some introductory instructions to the player. Type this:

```
print (' (type help to get a list of
  actions) ')
print (hero.name, 'enters a dark cave,
  searching for adventure. You will
  soon face the', monster.name)
```

We use a while loop to keep the game running until hero or monster health drops to 0. We then ask the player to choose a command: either `help`, `stats`, `explore`, `run` or `fight`.

Add this:

```
while hero.health > 0 and monster.
  health > 0:
  line = input('What do you want to
    do? >> ')
  if line in Commands.keys():
    Commands[line](hero,monster)
  else:
    print (hero.name, 'does not
      understand this suggestion.')
```

The only time this loop ends is on the death of the player or monster. So we will add this farewell *after* the loop:

```
print('Game over')
```

Run your program and debug all errors. Of course, nothing will happen as we have not written any content for our player methods. Check your file against the one provided online: *OOP_RPG_test.py*.

Building the methods

We will now build each of the methods we defined before but did not complete with any content.

The help method

We want this to simply print out the commands on one line. Replace the word pass in this method with:

```
print('Your choices are:')
for key in Commands.keys():
  print(key)
```

The stats method

We want to print out the current statistics for the player. Replace the word `pass` in this method with:

```
print('You are', self.name)
print('with health of', self.health)
print('your status is', self.status)
print(monster.name, 'health is',
  monster.health)
```

Try it!

Now try running the program and test if your help and stats methods are working correctly by choosing either the help or stats command when asked for your move. If you need it, a version completed to this point is provided as an online resource: *OOP_RPG_start.py*.

Three final methods are the heart of our gameplay.

We could invent many rules for these but here are some basic requirements we might use:

- `explore` could allow the player to gain health by resting and to confront monsters

- run could allow the player to escape a fight if health is low but could cost health points and allow a monster to gain health points by being left alone
- fight could cost players and monsters health points but allow them to win the game by defeating their opponent How could we code these methods?

The explore method

A neat way to decide if a monster comes on the scene is to toss a digital coin!

randint(0,1) will do this for us as it delivers only 0 or a 1. These equate to False and True in programming.

So writing if randint(0,1) is the same as saying 'do this only if we toss a 1'. Replace pass in your explore method now with:

```
self.heal()
print('Your health is now', self.
    health)
if randint(0, 1) == 1:
    print(monster.name, 'confronts you')
    print('What do you do?')
    self.status = 'confronted'
```

The run method

We need to penalise players for running away. One way to do that is to make people face the possibility of having to fight a monster. We will generate random numbers for both player and monster using their health. If the player number is smaller then they are forced to fight, otherwise we reduce player health and increase monster health:

Replace pass in your run method with:

```
if randint(0, self.health) < randint
    (0, monster.health):
    print('A monster has appeared')
    self.status = 'confronted'
    self.fight(monster)
else:
    self.tire()
    monster.heal()
    print('Your health suffered by
        running')
    print('Your health is now',
        self.health)
```

The fight method

Our approach will be to simulate a fight by using a random number function to reduce both player and monster health (fighting is exhausting!). If the player wins the battle they are rewarded with extra health. A drop to 0 or below will result in death.

We wrap all this in a loop that checks that the player has 'confronted' status. This variable is like the OK that a player is 'battle-ready'. This is set randomly in other methods to prevent players choosing to fight on every move.

Replace pass in your fight method with:

```
if self.status == 'confronted':
    self.hurt()
    monster.hurt()
    print(monster.name, 'attacks you')
    if self.health <= 0:
        print('You were killed by the',
            monster.name)
    elif monster.health > 0:
        print('You survived the', monster.
            name)
        print('Your health is now', self.
            health)
        self.status = 'normal'
    else:
        print('Victory! You defeated the',
            monster.name)
else:
    print('You are safe. Not a monster
        in sight anywhere!')
```

Run the game to debug. If you need help, a copy of this version is available online as a resource (*OOP_RPG_final.py*) as well as in a commented version.

A FURTHER TASK

The game works well enough, but it has a lot of room for improvements! Now you know about OOP and how the game operates, your task is to improve it by adding your own features or alter existing methods. Start by choosing from the following:

- Try changing some of the ways the random functions work in the methods.
- Include more than one life for the player.
- Try increasing the challenge of fights as time goes on by increasing a counter for each turn.
- Add an eating method with the risk of being found by the enemy.
- Add random pleasant events that increase points.
- Require two monsters to be eliminated. Have the second monster arrive after the first is killed.
- Swap monsters part way through the game.
- Have both monsters involved in the game at once.
- Add more feedback to players.
- Allow the player to find weapons when exploring to add to an inventory dictionary.
- Allow the player to select different weapons from the inventory to fight and vary levels of damage.
- Add other variables such as magic points.
- Add a time factor of day and night, say each minute, so that fights are more easily lost at night.
- Add geography so that the player moves to different areas and is safe in some of them.

9780170411820

THE TASK

Your task is to code two versions of the game of Nim. In the first version, a human player goes first and takes turns against the computer, which randomly chooses its moves. In the second version, the computer goes first and plays to win.

There are many ways to play the game of Nim or Sticks. In our version of the game we will start with one pile of any number of coins. Each player takes turns removing 1, 2 or 3 coins at a time. The person who takes the last coin loses the game.

For example, say there are five coins and Person A has the first move.

Person A takes one coin.

Person B takes three coins.

Person A loses, because they have been forced to take the last coin.

How can we work out the best way to play this game so that we can write a program to play it?

Defining

Play the game manually

1   First take turns playing the game with 10 coins, sticks or pens against an opponent.
2   Write down what you discover about strategies.

_____

_____

3   Does the player who goes first have an advantage or a disadvantage?

_____

4   Repeat the game starting with more than 10 coins.

5   Write down what you discover about strategies.

_____

_____

Using computational thinking to analyse the game

Let us imagine we go first, and assume our opponent will play their best possible move every time.

We will use the four stages of computational thinking we learnt in *Digital Technologies 7 & 8* to work through a solution to this problem.

- **Decomposition:** breaking down a big problem into smaller ones.
- **Pattern recognition:** discovering patterns in the data using data analysis.
- **Abstraction:** discovering and representing a main idea.
- **Designing algorithms:** creating a method for computer solution.

Web probe: Computational thinking

Follow the weblinks from the *Digital Technologies 9 & 10* website and watch these videos on computational thinking:

Video

- *Solving Problems at Google Using Computational Thinking*
- *CT at Google: Facilitating Software and Game Development through Abstraction*.

Explain how Google uses the concept of abstraction to help programmers develop games for mobile devices.

_____

_____

_____

_____

_____

_____

_____

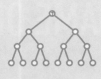
Suppose we start with four, three, or two coins. What should be our strategy?

If the pile has four coins, then if we take three, we force the opponent to take the last one.

If the pile has three coins, then if we take two, we force the opponent to take the last one.

If the pile has two coins, then if we take one, we force the opponent to take the last one.

So we can see a simple rule: when we have less than five coins, take *all* coins except the last one! Our opponent has to take the last coin and will lose.

Pattern recognition

The second stage of computational thinking is called *pattern recognition*. This involves finding patterns in data and making sense of data.

In this section we will see if we can discover a pattern for other numbers of coins.

Suppose that we started with five coins.

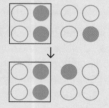

If we take one coin (leaving four), our opponent will take three – we lose.
If we take two coins (leaving three), our opponent will take two – we lose.
If we take three coins (leaving two), our opponent will take one – we lose.
No matter what we do when left with five coins, we lose.

9780170411820

Table 11.1 summarises the outcomes for five coins:

Table 11.1

If we take:	Our opponent will take:	Will we win or lose?
1	3	Lose
2	2	Lose
3	1	Lose

Our strategy should be: *There is no winning strategy!*
Next, suppose we started with six coins.

Complete this table summarising outcomes for six coins:

Table 11.2

If we take:	Our opponent will take:	Will we win or lose?
1	Same situation as described in last table	
2		
3		

Our strategy should be: *We should take _____ coins.*
Suppose we start with seven coins.

Complete this table summarising outcomes for seven coins:

Table 11.3

If we take:	Our opponent will take:	Will we win or lose?
1	1 – why?	
2		
3		

Our strategy should be: *We should take _____ coins.*
Suppose we start with eight coins.

9780170411820

Complete this table summarising outcomes for eight coins:

Table 11.4

If we take:	Our opponent will take:	Will we win or lose?
1		We lose – why?
2		
3		

Our strategy should be: *We should take* _____ *coins.*
Suppose we start with nine coins.

Complete this table summarising outcomes for nine coins:

Table 11.5

If we take:	Our opponent will take:	Will we win or lose?
1		
2		
3		

Our strategy should be: *We should take* _____ *coins.*
Suppose we start with 10 coins.

Complete this table summarising outcomes for 10 coins:

Table 11.6

If we take:	Our opponent will take:	Will we win or lose?
1		
2		
3		

Our strategy should be: *We should take* _____ *coins.*

9780170411820

Complete this table summarising the best strategy for differing numbers of coins by using data in previous tables:

Table 11.7

Number of coins in pile	We should take:	We would leave:	Do we win or lose?
1	1	0	lose
2	1	1	win
3	2	1	win
4	3	1	win
5	X	X	lose no matter what we take
6			
7			
8			
9	X	X	
10			
11			
12			
13			
14			
etc.			

Can you see a pattern?

Abstraction

The third stage of computational thinking is called *abstraction*. Abstraction turns something complex into something simpler by removing detail and reducing it to a general principle or main idea.

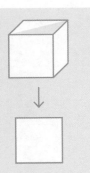

Ask yourself, which of the numbers of coins in the first column are losing numbers on your turn? That is, when the pile has that many coins and it is your move, you *cannot* win.

Conclusion: these are the numbers of coins we want our opponent to face on *their* turn!

Can you complete this rule? This rule, in the form of a simple algorithm, will be needed later when you develop Version 2.0 of this game.

If our opponent takes N coins, we should always take _____. If we go first we will always win using this strategy,

unless _____.

Algorithm design

The fourth and final stage in computational thinking is called *algorithm design*. This involves designing a series of ordered steps to solve a problem or achieve some end result, and refining these steps to enable a computer to find the solution.

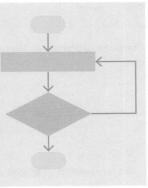

Use a flowchart or structured English to design a rule for automation by a computer to solve this problem. If you are not ready to do this yet, use the outline below to guide you.

Your task is now to develop a computer program using your class's chosen computer language to play the game, by building on the strategies you have discovered above using computational thinking.

We will do this in three stages: a first basic version to get the structure of our code, a second working version and a final version with added features.

Designing

Version 1.0 of Nim: without artificial intelligence

1 In the first version of the game a human player plays first and takes turns against the computer, which then randomly chooses a move. This version will be a prototype only. We will not yet use the data we collected to develop an intelligent algorithm for moves.

2 Complete this table of requirements.

Table 11.8

Requirement	Notes
Human player chooses number of coins	
Human plays first	
Identify player each move	
Player limited to one, two or three coins with error message otherwise	
Players cannot take more coins than in the pile or error message	
Computer opponent randomly selects one, two or three	
Message for win or lose	
Coins represented by printed asterisks	

3 Start by drawing a flowchart for your program using a starting pile of 10 objects. Use an asterisk or other symbol in your code to represent each coin in your output.

4 Have a friend check the logic of your flowchart.

Implementing

1 Start by writing out a structured English version of your flowchart.

2 Code your game using your class's chosen programming language.

3 Debug and refine your code.

Version 2.0 of Nim: with artificial intelligence

Now you will code some artificial intelligence for your computer! In the second version the computer goes first and plays to win!

Refer to Table 11.7 and the rule you devised following it to develop a strategy using computational thinking.

4 Complete Table 11.9 listing your requirements.

5 Use the same stages as you did for Version 1.0 to develop your code.

Table 11.9 Complete this table of requirements for Version 2.0 of the game, using data from Table 11.7 to code a strategy.

Requirements	Notes
Human player chooses number of coins	
Computer plays first (offer choice at start)	

Version 3.0 of Nim: Suggested improvements

6   Once you've completed Version 2.0 you may find you have further improvements to make to the game. Consider the following possible variations when you develop Version 3.0:
- Each player may take from one to four coins.
- The player who takes the last coin *wins*.
- There are two piles of coins. Each player may only take coins from one pile. The player taking last coin wins.
- Search online for other variations of Nim and select another version of the game to code.

7   What did you learn by completing this project?

_____

_____

_____

_____

_____

_____

9780170411820

8 Identify additional features you could include.

_____

_____

_____

_____

_____

_____

_____

Evaluating

1 Have two or three other classmates comment on your program and record their suggestions here.

_____

_____

_____

_____

_____

_____

_____

_____

2 Suggest improvements to your program.

_____

_____

_____

_____

_____

_____

_____

_____

_____

9780170411820

THE TASK

You have learnt that the first stage in computational thinking is *decomposition*. One decomposition technique is called *recursion*.

After finding out a little about Fibonacci numbers and recursion, your task will be to program a spreadsheet to generate Fibonacci numbers using both iteration and recursion and to compare these different approaches.

Your final challenge in this project will be to achieve the same result using your coding skills and a general-purpose programming language.

Understanding recursion

Recursion describes problems that can be broken down into simpler versions of the same problem – a bit like a tree branch where a stem either branches into two new ones, which again themselves branch or else grows a leaf and terminates.

Let's say you are in row G of a theatre and want to know how many people are in the audience. Imagine that anyone can count the people in their own row but no one wants to stand up to count other rows. (See Figure 12.1.)

Figure 12.1 Using recursion to count a theatre audience. Person in row A eventually reports 7 as number of people in their row to person behind them in row B. They also have 7 so now the total is 14 and is reported to person in row C who adds 8 to give 22 and so on back to row G. What total do they have reported to them?

One solution would be to ask a person in front in row F to find the total from row F down. They might then ask a person in front of them for the total from their row down … and so on until row A was reached. The person in row A could then tell row B how many in row A so that row B could now tell row C the total for rows A and B. Row C tells row D the total for rows A to C, and so on until it got back to you in row G. Now you simply add your own row and you have the audience total. You didn't need to move! The algorithm we used here is an example of recursion.

Skill builder: Summing using recursion

Write an algorithm for the theatre recursion example using both a flowchart and structured English.

Skill builder

Recursion and Fibonacci

Perhaps you have heard of Fibonacci numbers. They are named after Leonardo of Pisa who wrote about them in 1202 AD (Figure 12.2).

Figure 12.2 Leonardo of Pisa was the son (*filius*) of the Bonacci family and hence became known as Fibonacci.

Fibonacci numbers are a sequence of integers formed where every one after the first two is the sum of the two preceding ones:

0, 1, 1, 2, 3, 5, 8, 13, etc.

If you were asked to find the 10th Fibonacci number, you would need to know the two preceding ones and then to find those you would need the two before them and so on. To find any higher Fibonacci number you need all those before it. Again, we have encountered a recursion algorithm.

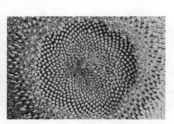

Clockwise top left: Shutterstock.com/andersphoto; Dreamstime.com/Draftmode; Shutterstock.com/Eric Isselee; Shutterstock.com/Stefano Buttafoco

Figure 12.3 Well-known examples of the natural world showing Fibonacci sequences in action.

INFOBIT: RECURSION

A joke popular among programmers is that in order to understand recursion, you must first understand recursion! Another joke is that people go through three stages learning recursion:

First, they hate it because they can't understand it.
Then, they love it because they finally understand it.
Finally, they hate it again because they decide it's inefficient!

Web probe: Fibonacci

Can you imagine a maths video having millions of views?! Follow the weblink from the *Digital Technologies 9 & 10* website to view the video *Doodling in Math: Spirals, Fibonacci and Being a Plant*.

Video

Defining

1   Describe what the connection is between the Fibonacci numbers and each of the following:

Table 12.1

pine cone	
sunflower plant	
golden rectangle	
nautilus shell	
Parthenon	

2   Complete this table of the first 10 Fibonacci numbers. We have chosen the index of the first number to be 0 (a common programming practice).

Table 12.2

Index	0	1	2	3	4	5	6	7	8	9	10
Fibonacci number	0	1	1	2							

9780170411820

Designing

You already know the method of iteration from previous programming. Iteration occurs when code repeats. We can make a spreadsheet do this by using the Fill down tool. We will include this iterative approach here under the heading Designing, as our final goal is to implement a recursive function.

Using iteration

1. Create an empty spreadsheet using Excel or Google Sheets.
2. Write the heading 'index' in cell A1 and 'Fibonacci(index)' in cell B1. We have written Fibonacci(index) in the form of a function, in preparation for coding it later.
3. Fill down integers 0 to 30 in column A as the index column beginning with 0 in cell A2 and 1 in cell A3.
4. Now start off column B by entering the first two Fibonacci numbers: 0 in cell B2 and 1 in cell B3.
5. Enter the formula =B2+B3 in cell B4. (See Figure 12.4.)
6. Fill down this formula to reach integer 30 in column A. (See Figure 12.5.)
7. Was there any delay calculating index 30? Complete the values in Table 12.3:

Table 12.3

Index	28	29	30
Fibonacci(index)			

8. Check by hand that the last number equals the sum of the two before it.

	A	B
1	index	Fibonacci(index)
2	0	0
3	1	1
4	2	=B2+B3
5	3	
6	4	

Figure 12.4 Enter the formula

	A	B
1	index	Fibonacci(index)
2	0	0
3	1	1
4	2	1
5	3	2
6	4	3
7	5	5
8	6	8
9	7	13
10	8	21

Figure 12.5 First 10 rows after the Fill down using iterative formula

Microsoft Corporation

Using recursion

Here is a recursive function for Fibonacci written in structured English for Fibonacci(index).

```
IF index < 2 THEN
   fibonacci(index)=index
ELSE
   fibonacci(index)= fibonacci(index-1)+ fibonacci(index-2)
```

Notice that a recursive algorithm makes *a call back to itself*. This can be difficult to understand.

Can you trace through this algorithm starting with an index value of 4? Describe what happens in detail here.

_____

_____

_____

_____

_____

_____

_____

_____

In Figure 12.6 on the next page, the only Fibonacci numbers we know already are the ones that are shaded: the first two Fibonacci numbers, 0 and 1. Observe that FIB(0) and FIB(1) are the only boxes whose values are known. Inspect the diagram and trace how FIB(4) is found by moving down the tree, and then up again.

In order to find out what the answer to Fibonacci(4) is, we are forced to descend the tree to lower branches coming from it, just as we did in the example of the theatre at the beginning of this project, until we reach values we know.

We keep unpacking the problem until we eventually reach ones that are shaded (just like the leaves at the ends of branches), whose values we know, and so we now change direction and ascend the tree again using addition to find each higher value, until we eventually reach the top of the tree with the solution to Fibonacci(4).

When tracing recursive functions, there is a descending and ascending part. The 'descending' part occurs as the recursion asks questions for which the answers are lower down, so it heads to these (which are known). The 'ascending' part occurs when the recursion rises up to the starting point again carrying these answers. This is like you finding your relationship to an ancestor many generations before by asking repeatedly 'who is your father?' until you reach that person high up in the family tree who then reports back down to you again.

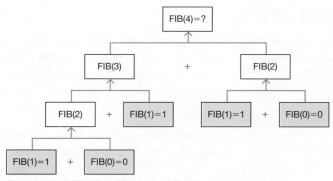

Figure 12.6 Finding Fibonacci(4) using recursion

Implementing

The first three steps are provided for both Excel and Google Sheets.

1   In Excel (Win or Mac), open and save a new spreadsheet and make sure you save it as an Excel Macro-Enabled Worksheet, otherwise your code will not run.
    In Google Sheets open and save a new spreadsheet.
2   In Excel, select the Developer tab (if not visible turn it on under Preferences > Ribbon and Toolbar). Select Macros. Name the new module, click the '+'.
    Delete any default code already present and type the code shown in Figure 12.7 into the empty window.
    If using Google Sheets, under the Tools menu select Script Editor and type the code shown in Figure 12.8 and save it (important!).
3   Close the editing window and fill column A as previously with the index values 1 to 30.
4   In B2 type = Fibonacci(A2). You should notice your newly defined Fibonacci user-defined function will appear. You have created your own Excel function just for this spreadsheet!
5   Fill down your Fibonacci function to index 20 only. It will now generate the Fibonacci numbers using recursion.
    Warning! The following final steps may freeze your spreadsheet. Make sure you know how to force quit an application on your computer! Both Excel and Google Sheets will use the process illustrated in Figure 12.6 to calculate each Fibonacci number. Google Sheets server allows a maximum time for calculations of 30 seconds, so it will probably stop at some point.
6   Have a stopwatch ready. Now fill down your Fibonacci formula one row at a time to index 23. Complete the values in Table 12.4 and the time each one took.

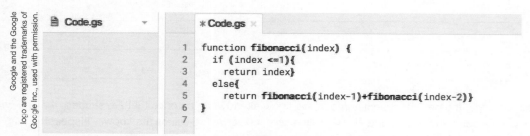

Figure 12.7 Creating a user-defined spreadsheet function in Excel's Visual Basic

```
Function fibonacci(index)
    If index <= 1 Then
        fibonacci = index
    Else
        fibonacci = fibonacci(index - 1) + fibonacci(index - 2)
    End If
End Function
```

```
1   function fibonacci(index) {
2     if (index <=1){
3       return index}
4     else{
5       return fibonacci(index-1)+fibonacci(index-2)}
6   }
7
```

Figure 12.8 Creating a user-defined recursive function using JavaScript in Google Sheets

9780170411820

Table 12.4

Index	21	22	23
Fibonacci(index)			
Time taken (sec)			

7 Fill the formula down to cell B32 and time how long it takes to complete these rows. Then try even higher index values. A solution is provided in the online resources on the *Digital Technologies 9 & 10* website if you need help.

Evaluating

1 Why is this formula so slow when calculating higher index values?

_____

_____

_____

_____

_____

_____

_____

_____

_____

Comparing iteration and recursion algorithms

Here again is our algorithm using *iteration* written in structured English for finding Fibonacci(index).

```
prev=0
current=1
count=2
IF index<2 THEN
  fibonacci(index)=index
ELSE
  WHILE count<=index DO
    new=prev+current
    prev=current
    current=new
    count=count+1
  ENDWHILE
  fibonacci(index)=current
```

Here is our algorithm using *recursion* as used in the last section, written in structured English.

```
IF index < 2 THEN
  fibonacci(index)=index
ELSE
  fibonacci(index)= fibonacci(index-1)+ fibonacci(index-2)
```

2 When comparing iteration and recursion, programmers have said that mathematicians prefer recursion and programmers prefer iteration. Can you explain this and do you agree?

_____

_____

_____

_____

_____

_____

_____

3 Can you find any other algorithms for calculating Fibonacci numbers?

_____

_____

_____

_____

_____

PROGRAMMING CHALLENGE 1

Write a program that asks the user for a number then prints the Fibonacci number corresponding to that index. The program is to calculate the Fibonacci number twice, by using both iteration and recursion.

A solution written in Python is provided in the online resources on the _Digital Technologies 9 & 10_ website. See _fib_iteration_recursion.py_. Add a timing function to print time taken to calculate the Fibonacci number using each method. To see this difference you will need to ask for a number with index greater than 30.

PROGRAMMING CHALLENGE 2

In mathematics, the factorial value of an integer is the product of all positive integers less than or equal to it.

So factorial 5 (written in maths as 5!) is:

$= 5 \times 4 \times 3 \times 2 \times 1$

$= 120$

and 4! is:

$= 4 \times 3 \times 2 \times 1$

$= 24$

Create a spreadsheet that uses both iteration and recursion to generate factorials of integers from 1 to 50.

Skill builder: Fun with recursion!

In Chapter 23 in _Digital Technologies 7 & 8_, reference was made to using the Ozobot robot to perform recursion.

Skill builder

Now you understand recursion, follow the weblink from the _Digital Technologies 9 & 10_ website for 'Challenge lesson: Ozobot Bit – the Fibonacci Traveler'.

Weblink

You will need to print the path template provided from the online challenge lesson. Use the code provided online as a resource with this text and open it via the Ozoblockly website. Load it into your Ozobot.

Your task is then to run it and explain what the code does and how it uses recursion.

9780170411820

PROJECT: MILLIONAIRE BY 30?

THE TASK

How long would it take to become a millionaire if you invested $100 now at a compound interest rate of 10% per annum, and not make withdrawals? This project will investigate this problem and then apply the skills acquired to Moore's Law.

Planning

Problems needing the mathematics of compound interest are very common. You may have come across some in your maths class. It is used to work out house repayments, the spread of viruses, bacterial growth and radioactive decay.

Spreadsheets can be used to simulate real life problems such as these and they have a built-in tool called a Goal Seeker, which can even predict the future!

You may have solved the famous chessboard problem using a spreadsheet in *Digital Technologies 7 & 8*, Chapter 12. This project uses a similar technique of *iteration* and introduces the important technique of *goal seeking*.

Figure 13.1 Compound interest is interest applied to the original amount and also on the accumulated interest of previous periods.

INFOBIT

The formula for compound interest is written as:
$$A = P(1 + r/100)^n$$
Which gives the total value of an investment of P dollars at r% p.a. after n years.

Knowledge probe: Compound interest

Let us look at how an amount of $100 can grow if invested at 10% per annum interest rate. At the end of year 1 you will have the original $100 invested plus 10% extra. So at the end year 1:

$100 + $100 × 0.10

= $100 × 1.10

= $110.00

Similarly, at the start of year 2 you now have $110 invested. So at the end of year 2:

$110 × 1.10

= $121.00

Similarly at the end year 3:

$121 × 1.10

= $133.10

And so on …

Each year the amount from the end of the previous year is multiplied by 1.10 to get the next year's total amount. How rich will you be by the end of year 100? By the end of this project you will have created a tool to answer this question – and more!

Designing

1 Add headings on Columns A, B, C, D and G as shown in Figure 13.2.

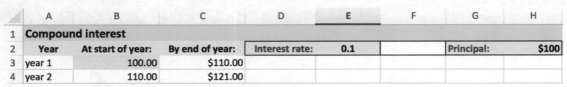

	A	B	C	D	E	F	G	H
1	Compound interest							
2	Year	At start of year:	By end of year:	Interest rate:	0.1		Principal:	$100
3	year 1	100.00	$110.00					
4	year 2	110.00	$121.00					

Figure 13.2 Column headings for millionaire spreadsheet

2 In E2, write an interest rate expressed as a decimal (make it 0.10, which represents 10%). The part of the formula using this interest rate will need an absolute cell reference. Can you explain why? Make sure you understand the difference between absolute and relative cell references.

3 In H2, write the principal (make it $100 to start with).

4 Consecutively, label 100 rows down column A as shown, each with 'year n'.
(Hint: Write the first two manually, then select these and use Fill Down. Your spreadsheet will complete the pattern.)

5 In B3, enter the formula =H2, to record the first year's principal correctly (which is in cell H2).

6 In cell C3, write the formula:

    =B3*(1+E2)

In other words, multiply last year's total by itself plus interest. This was the pattern we discovered in the Planning phase earlier. Explain the reason for the $ signs.

7 Fill down this formula to the 100th year.

8 In cell B4, enter the formula:

    =C3

9 Fill down column B to the 100th year.

10 At which year does your amount exceed $1 000 000?
If you did it correctly, the answer should be at the end of the 97th year!

11 Check this using this mathematical formula and a calculator.
A = P(1 + r/100)^n, where P = $100, r=10 and n=97.

Implementing

A hundred years is a long time, and you are unlikely to be alive to see your money, despite medical advances! What would we have to invest as principal to make $1 000 000 within 30 years?

Goal seeking

Goal seeking is a great tool for exploring different scenarios and for answering this problem!

1 Choose Tools > Goal Seek from the menu bar or from Data > What-If Analysis > Goal Seek and use the following values:
   • Enter the goal cell reference: here cell C32
   • Enter goal value: here $1 000 000
   • Enter the cell we are allowing to be changed to achieve our goal: here (the principal) cell H2 (see Figure 13.3).

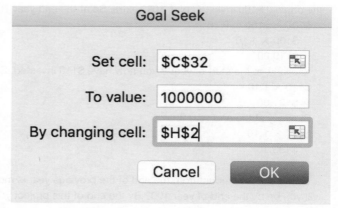

Figure 13.3 Goal seeking for millions

Evaluation

1 Goal seeking is quite exciting as you can see figures rippling down the spreadsheet as the calculation proceeds – a rare example of the time taken by the computer for the many recalculations involved. Now improve the appearance of your spreadsheet by adding formatting features.

2 Invent two other questions to ask and solve them using the power of goal seeking.

9780170411820

Taking it further: Moore or less?

Gordon Moore of Intel (Figure 13.4) devised a famous rule now known as Moore's Law.

He claimed the number of transistors in an integrated circuit (chip) doubles approximately every two years. There were 2300 transistors on a chip in 1971.

Figure 13.4 Gordon Moore of Intel, who observed what is now known as Moore's Law.

INFOBIT

In 1976 Gordon Moore said: 'We are bringing about the next great revolution in the history of mankind – the transition to the electronic age.'

He started Intel with Robert Noyce and Andrew Grove in 1968. Intel has since become the world's most successful semiconductor manufacturer.

1 If Moore's Law is true, what should the number of transistors on a chip be now? Set up a spreadsheet to solve this for the years 1971–2030. Note down the number you get for this year.

2 Find out the rough number of transistors possible on a chip produced now. How close did you come? Was your prediction under or over?

3 Add a column to complete the actual numbers for at least every decade since 1970.

4 Do you think in 1971 George Moore was bold to make such a prediction?

5 Do you think his law could continue indefinitely? Is it accurate to call it a law?

6 If there is a limit to the number of transistors that can fit on a chip of a certain size, what would cause such a limit?

7 Research the advances being made in chip manufacture that are likely to affect Moore's Law.

THE TASK

Your task is to create a spreadsheet to help your student council organise an invitation-only end-of-school dance. You have decided to design it so other schools can use it for their events.

You should have completed Guided project: Using spreadsheets in Chapter 11 of *Digital Technologies 7 & 8* before starting this project.

Figure 14.1

- Your spreadsheet will work out costs linked to the number of guests.
- Some costs depend on the number of guests that accept invitations. Your spreadsheet will automatically update these.
- Some items have fixed costs, such as security, DJ or a slushie machine. These costs will be included.
- You have been told that printed invitations are to be designed and mailed to all students who will receive tickets only if they accept via email.
- Your spreadsheet should keep track of who is coming.
- You should provide a summary in each cost category.
- You should use colour in cells to warn if expenses reach above your budget.

Defining

1. Decide your overall budget.
2. Decide the various categories of items needed for the dance. Consider such things as invitations (if printed), food, decorations, hiring (slushie machine, jukebox, photobooth, DJ, etc.).
3. Decide the maximum and minimum numbers of guests.

4. Decide categories for expenses. Split the overall budget into the separate categories.
5. Some categories will be one-off costs (decorations, slushie machine) and others will depend on the number of guests (food and drink). List these clearly.

Designing

1. What features will you include in your spreadsheet that will make it useful and easy to use. For example, the amounts in the total boxes could change to red when they exceed their budgeted amount. This will require conditional formatting.
2. Sketch on paper a design for the layout of your spreadsheet. See Figure 14.2 for an example.
3. Make up test values for later checking of your final working spreadsheet.

Implementing

Formulas should link the cell containing the total number of guests to cells requiring quantities of things.

1. Enter items in all sections: Guests, Music, Decorations, Food and drinks, Other. Leave other columns empty for now. Fill in the Budget cell with an upper amount for the total dance cost. Fill in the cost per item in the last column.
2. You decide to serve food in buffet style, so it is not sensible to calculate food and drink costs per person. Instead, use a formula to work out how many groups of 10 people there are and a formula to round up fractions. Food and drink can be ordered for every 10 guests or part thereof. Why would we round up rather than round to the nearest integer?

_____

_____

_____

If cell D8 contains the total number of guests, then the formula =ROUNDUP(D8/10,0) will work out how many groups of 10 and round this up to the nearest integer. The 0 in the formula rounds the answer to 0 decimal places (i.e. the nearest integer). For example, if there are 34 guests, then 3.4 will be rounded to 4. Link the cell containing the total number of guests to food and drink requirements using this ROUNDUP formula.

9780170411820

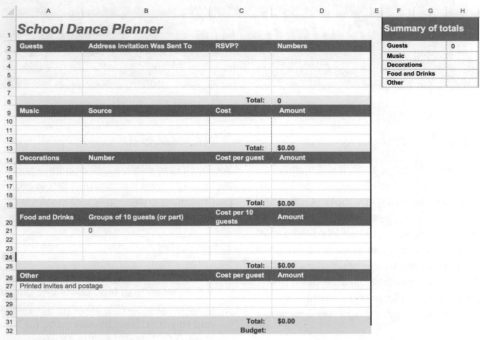

	A	B	C	D	E	F	G	H
	School Dance Planner					**Summary of totals**		
2	Guests	Address Invitation Was Sent To	RSVP?	Numbers		Guests	0	
3						Music		
4						Decorations		
5						Food and Drinks		
6						Other		
7								
8			Total:	0				
9	Music	Source	Cost	Amount				
10								
11								
12								
13			Total:	$0.00				
14	Decorations	Number	Cost per guest	Amount				
15								
16								
17								
18								
19			Total:	$0.00				
20	Food and Drinks	Groups of 10 guests (or part)	Cost per 10 guests	Amount				
21		0						
22								
23								
24								
25			Total:	$0.00				
26	Other		Cost per guest	Amount				
27	Printed invites and postage							
28								
29								
30								
31			Total:	$0.00				
32			Budget:					

Figure 14.2

3 Enter invited guest names and numbers to test your spreadsheet.
4 Add the summary table for the categories in another section of the spreadsheet.
5 Add conditional formatting to alert you to running over budget.

Evaluating

1 Check the spreadsheet is working correctly by entering invented values.
2 Improve your spreadsheet and make it more user-friendly.
3 Test the spreadsheet yourself and have others test it and suggest improvements.
4 What did you learn from this project?

_____

_____

_____

_____

_____

_____

_____

5 Identify additional features you could include.

_____

_____

_____

_____

_____

_____

_____

_____

_____

_____

Repeating the design cycle

It is not often that a design cycle is performed only once. Improvements will mean that a programmer will need to work through the process again.

Here are some suggested improvements to try:
• Add a section for the program of events through the night.
• Add a section for income with charges to guests for tickets.
• Add features of your own.

THE *GAME OF LIFE*

The *Game of Life* is not really a game at all. It is a 'cellular automaton' and was invented by Cambridge mathematician John Conway. It is great for illustrating the topic of modelling and simulation.

The game consists of a collection of filled-in squares that, based on a few mathematical rules, can live, die or multiply. After starting the game, black squares either die, are created or simply stay alive. The game can be simulated using grid paper, pencil and eraser. Every cell has eight neighbours, which may be horizontally, vertically or diagonally adjacent.

Game rules

For any square that is 'populated' (shaded in):

- If a square has *one or no* neighbours it dies, as if by loneliness.
- If a square has *four or more* neighbours it dies, as if by overpopulation.
- If a square has *two or three* neighbours, it survives.

For any space that is 'unpopulated' (empty):

- Each square with *three* neighbours becomes populated.

   Check the patterns below in Figure 15.1 and see how this 10 generation sequence obeys the rules above by working through each generation carefully.

THE TASK

Your task is to explore this algorithm and then decide how well it might model actual population growth. A further programming challenge is to write code to reproduce the *Game of Life*'s rules.

Planning

1 Follow the weblink from the *Digital Technologies 9 & 10* website to read about and play the *Game of Life*. (Alternatively, you can download an app to your device by searching for 'Conway's Game of Life'.) Set up the starting population shown in Figure 15.1 then step through 10 generations. Note the generation counter.

2 Research how John Conway first came to invent this game and summarise this here.

Weblink

_____

_____

_____

_____

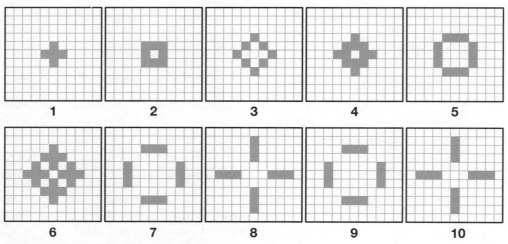

Figure 15.1 Ten generations, starting with a small cross

Designing

1 Experiment with the predefined patterns on the website's drop-down menu. Record what happens to each of the population patterns using Table 15.1.

2 Now invent more of your own patterns, sketching them in the grids below. Then, test them. Choose a favourite pattern. How many generations does it last before it becomes still or disappears?

_____

What happens most often: do generations mostly die out, stay still, grow larger or endlessly alternate between patterns?

_____

_____

For the following you need to refer to the large collection at the *Game of Life* Lexicon. Follow the weblink from the *Digital Technologies 9 & 10* website.

Weblink

3 Can you find a starting pattern that always dies out, no matter how many separate organisms there are to start with?

_____

4 Can you find a pattern that stays exactly the same for every generation?

_____

5 Can you find a pattern that oscillates between two patterns, that is, a pattern that changes to another in the first step and then changes back to itself?

_____

6 Look for the following well-known patterns in the lexicon and write what happens to each over time by completing Table 15.1.
- The pulsar
- Blinker
- Toad
- A glider

Table 15.1

Pattern name of initial population	Description of what happened over time

Invent your own seed population patterns and sketch them here!

Implementing

Class activity: Winning pattern

The class challenge is to find the starting pattern that lasts through the most generations before it stays still or dies out.

Draw the winner's starting population here.

Evaluating

1   Class discussion or personal reflection: do you think the *Game of Life* mathematical simulation is anything like real population growth in living organisms? Summarise the class conclusions.

_____

_____

_____

_____

_____

2   Suggest modifications to the algorithm that could achieve a more accurate simulation of population growth.

_____

_____

_____

_____

_____

3   Write a response to the following statement by Paul Callahan:

> We can see that [the Game of] Life, simple as it is to describe, exhibits much of the complexity of our own universe.
>
> Paul Callahan, 'What is the Game of Life?' (Math.com)

_____

_____

_____

_____

_____

4   What did you learn from this project?

_____

_____

_____

_____

_____

5   Can you find other examples online of mathematical simulations such as this?

_____

_____

_____

_____

_____

_____

PROGRAMMING CHALLENGE

1   Write a program, using x and y coordinates and your programming language's array structure, to print a 12 × 12 grid of each of the first 10 generations for any starting pattern.

2   For the board use 0s in place of empty cells and 1s for cells that are filled. First decide what you want to happen at the edges of the board.

THE TASK

Australia played a major role in the development of the United Nations Universal Declaration of Human Rights. Your task is to produce a multimedia product to illustrate one of its 30 statements. Your product will be combined with those of other groups in your class. Treat this task as a commission given to you as a digital designer.

Figure 16.1 United Nations logo; artist's interpretation; protesters exercising their right to peaceful association (Article 20 of the Universal Declaration of Human Rights).

Defining

1 Form a group of three to four people.
2 Find a copy of the Universal Declaration of Human Rights online. Search for a simplified version if you prefer that to the original.
3 Research how these 30 articles came to be agreed upon by all countries at the United Nations General Assembly following the Second World War and find out what Australia's role was in their creation. This research should be presented briefly in your presentation in some way. Choose one of the articles to focus on.

4 Before starting any work on a digital project, it is essential to know who the target audience is and what their needs are. Think about how users will be helped or affected by your product. Decide the audience and needs.
5 It is important that your group not only understands and agrees exactly what they are doing, but also agrees on the project interface. In the designing stage you will design the interface, but at this stage it is important to decide its features and discuss it.
6 What form will your project take? Will it be a website? A movie? An animation?

To gain inspiration, follow the weblinks from the *Digital Technologies 9 & 10* website to watch the videos listed below.
- *My Last Day*, a video by Amnesty International.
- *The Universal Declaration of Human Rights*, a video by the Human Rights Action Center.

Video

7 How will you acquire images, video, animation, audio, text? Will you use interactivity?
8 Decide roles. Typical multimedia roles include: project manager, creative director, creative team, programmer.

Designing

1 Choose a tool for authoring the project. Here are some suggestions:
- movie (e.g. Premiere, iMovie)
- animation (e.g. Flash, PowToon, Edge Animate)
- presentation: slides or schematic (e.g. PowerPoint, Prezi, Google Presentation, Keynote)
- web authoring (e.g. online templates: WordPress, Weebly, Squarespace; web authoring: Adobe Muse)
- other: Adobe Spark, Nutshell phone app.
2 If you are planning an interactive product, consider these possibilities: hyperlinks, words as navigational buttons on your home page, animated text, graphics with slow reveals, videos that loop.
3 Create a storyboard. Consider using a tool such as PowerPoint or Google Presentation for your storyboard.
4 Build a prototype of your project. A prototype is a basic but incomplete model of a project. Include rough screen designs for scenes with placeholders for text, graphics, audio, video and animation.

5 Test the prototype on other members of the class and ask your teacher for their views.

6 Use the graphical user interface (GUI) principles summarised below to guide you in designing the appearance of your product and its interface.

Implementing

1 Acquire all assets.

2 Build the project.

Evaluating

There are three main types of testing used in developing multimedia projects.

- *Interface testing* asks users to comment on prototypes early in the project, and then later to suggest improvements to the design.
- *Navigation testing* makes sure that all links go to the right places.
- *Functional testing* checks if the product meets the original design specifications.

1 Test the product within your group and then on other members of your class. Ask your teacher for their opinions. Make changes as required.

2 Optional: present the final project to the class.

3 What did you learn from this project?

_____

_____

_____

_____

_____

_____

_____

4 Identify additional features that could be included.

_____

_____

_____

_____

_____

_____

GUI design principles

Keep the following GUI guidelines in mind when working on your project.

- Consistency: users expect that different applications will have similarities, which means that knowledge about one product is transferable to another. Consistency in screen design is one of the most important principles of all.
- Manipulation: people like to be in charge of their actions. Have your product pause and await user interaction.
- Intuitiveness: actions and navigation should be easily understood. A user should not have to consult a manual.
- Feedback: a click on a button should result in some response showing clearly that the action has taken place. A sound or a change in the appearance of a button is important.
- Forgiveness: if users make mistakes, they should be able to undo them and not be locked away to a screen from which it is difficult to return.
- Aesthetics: the design should be appealing to users. Objects should not be cluttered on the screen. White space is important and too much text should be avoided. The colours chosen should be planned in advance. This is known as a colour palette. Visit the Adobe Color website for an extensive selection. Follow the weblink from the *Digital Technologies 9 & 10* website.
- Functionality: navigation should be clear, and commonly used buttons should be easily accessible.
- Voice: which person or voice will you use? A multimedia title written in the first person ('I') makes the user feel part of the action, as in an interactive game. The second person ('you') makes the user feel they are part of a conversation. The third person ('they') suggests authority but less involvement.

Weblink

9780170411820

PROJECT: CREATE YOUR OWN AUGMENTED REALITY PRODUCT

THE TASK

Your task will be to create a complete interactive multimedia product in the form of a small booklet or set of A4 posters that trigger augmented reality (AR) experiences. We suggest you use Aurasma, or a similar app to author your project. Images in your book will act as triggers for augmented content, which may be images, video, text, websites or audio.

Although this project is written for a group, it can just as easily be completed individually. Your teacher will brainstorm possible themes with you.

Some ideas to get started:

- Anti-bullying posters that trigger videos/animations.
- Modern images of ruins that trigger reconstructed ancient ruins.
- Images of elements of the periodic table that trigger examples of their uses.
- Images of different landmarks around the world that trigger the names of the cities where they are located, presented as a quiz.
- Famous works of art of sculptures that trigger images and biographies of the artists.
- Mathematical questions that trigger worked solutions.
- Selection from the 30 UN Declaration of Human Rights in form of posters triggering video/animations bringing them to life (see Chapter 16).
- Bring a timeline to life (topic from course, history, invention, science, civilisations).

Figure 17.1 Creating an AR timeline

INFOBIT: AR IN 1901!

In 1901, L Frank Baum (author of *The Wizard of Oz*) in his book *The Master Key* imagined augmented reality 112 years before the invention of Google Glasses! It is the earliest recorded reference to this idea.

Mixed reality

AR is just one part of a range of mixed reality digital experiences beginning with our real world and ending with completely virtual digital experiences such as video games played using virtual reality (VR) glasses, such as Oculus Rift (see Figure 17.2).

MIXED REALITY (MR)

| Real environment | Augmented reality (AR) | Augmented virtuality (AV) | Virtual environment |

Figure 17.2 The continuum of mixed realities

At the extreme left of Figure 17.2 on the previous page is the real world and to the right are the completely artificial worlds we can create using computers. From left to right: the real world; augmented reality (the spacecraft is seen on the mobile device as if really there); augmented virtuality (the weatherman is superimposed over a virtual map) and finally virtual reality (where the user participates in a virtual world, perhaps as an avatar).

See if you can experience a VR app using a device similar to those shown in Figure 17.3. The phone app Within is a good place to start. Follow the weblink from the *Digital Technologies 9 & 10* website.

Weblink

How does AR work?

Augmented reality works by taking inputs (or 'triggers') from the environment such as features in an image or a marker and using these as anchors on which to overlay digital outputs (or 'expressions') onto a real-world view seen through the device. These overlays may include images, audio, web pages or vibrations (haptic).

1 Use the Internet to find out how overlays are connected to their trigger images in AR.

_____

_____

_____

_____

_____

_____

_____

_____

_____

_____

_____

_____

Figure 17.3 (top to bottom) Using any smartphone, VR can be viewed through low-cost cardboard glasses. Other products such as Samsung's Gear VR provide added features and at the high end, Oculus Rift is controlled using a powerful PC.

2 Use the Internet to find at least one application of AR for each of the following industries: medicine, tourism, military and marketing.

_____

_____

_____

_____

_____

_____

_____

_____

_____

_____

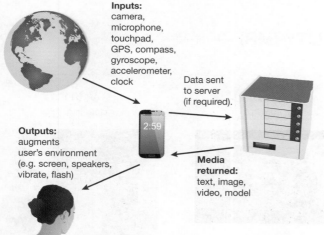

Inputs:
camera, microphone, touchpad, GPS, compass, gyroscope, accelerometer, clock

Data sent to server (if required).

Outputs:
augments user's environment (e.g. screen, speakers, vibrate, flash)

Media returned:
text, image, video, model

Figure 17.4 Augmented reality works by taking inputs (or 'triggers') from the environment

9780170411820

Download
Aurasma

Focus on the image

Watch it come to life

Figure 17.5 This poster by James Pearson was a winner in a NSW Youth Week poster competition. Here it is the trigger for an AR Aura using the Aurasma app. Test it out by downloading Aurasma on your phone and viewing this image. A small image of the Youth Week website will appear and tapping it will load the web page.

Defining

1   Form groups of three to four people and use the Internet to find a definition of AR and explain the difference between VR and AR.

_____

_____

_____

_____

2   Find out how AR works and briefly summarise this.

_____

_____

_____

_____

_____

Weblink

3   Download the HP Reveal phone/tablet app and use it to create your own AR experience by clicking on the '+' symbol and following the instructions.

In your group, discuss reasons for using AR. They may include the following:

- delivering objects without needing the life-sized object to be actually there
- modifications or additions to an original object or view of the object (such as 2D objects becoming when viewed with AR app)
- showing an object functioning without needing to operate it
- teaching about an object.

Weblink

4   Visit the HP Reveal Studio website and create an account. The excellent user guide will teach you to create your first AR experience (called Auras in Aurasma) as you perform the following steps in order:

- login to the Aurasma Studio website and select *My Auras*
- select + *Create New Aura*
- select *Create Trigger Image* then click *Next*
- select *Click to Upload Overlay* and save it
- resize and position the overlay (see Figure 17.6)
- test using *Preview*
- click *Save* and make sure you leave it on 'Public' setting.

Try it out using the Aurasma phone app.

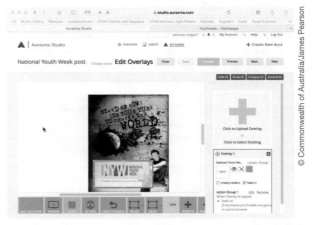

Figure 17.6 Setting up an overlay over the trigger image

5   Decide on a concept for your project product. This may need to be modified as you progress – ideas are often too ambitious and time runs out!

6   Choose a media type for triggers (input): printed booklet, poster(s), cards, worksheets, real objects.

7   Choose a media type for expressions/overlays (output): images, movies, 3D objects (more challenging).

8   Write out a statement describing your goals for your AR product.

9 Appoint members of the group to roles such as:
- producer
- designer
- author
- programmer.

Designing

1 Have one person create a storyboard for the project for the group to discuss, modify and finally agree upon.
2 Collect ideas for media assets (both the triggers and overlays).
3 Collect or create the images and/or videos required.
4 Design and create other content such as text.
5 Create all triggers and overlays.

Implementing

1 Prepare printed material as required.
2 Use AR software such as Aurasma Studio to assemble your AR product.

Evaluating

1 Have your group test the product and then invite a range of users to test it. Do not try to influence their testing. It is often best to move outside and have them make notes.
2 Ask:
- Is the material presented accurately and with sufficient detail?
- Is the user interface well designed?
- Does the project work well technically?
- Does the use of AR enhance understanding?
- Does the use of AR enhance the user experience?
Summarise users' feedback below.

_____

_____

_____

_____

_____

_____

_____

_____

_____

3 What did you learn from this project?

_____

_____

_____

_____

_____

_____

_____

_____

_____

_____

_____

_____

_____

4 What would you do differently?

_____

_____

_____

_____

_____

_____

_____

_____

_____

_____

9780170411820

HTML

Knowledge probe: What is HTML?

Hypertext Markup Language (HTML) is code used to structure and display a web page and its content. It has existed since the first day of the World Wide Web and the first browser.

Knowledge Probe

HTML is not a programming language but a *markup language*, because it consists of tags, not control structures, which describe how a browser displays any text positioned between the tags.

HTML essentials

Paired HTML tags

HTML code can be used to make words bold, define a paragraph, provide a link to a URL or perhaps fetch and deliver images to the page.

Most HTML tags are written as *pairs* of tags. Here is an example:

```
<p>HTML code is very useful.</p>
```

This tag pair has defined a paragraph. We can even nest tags inside other tags:

```
<p>HTML code is <strong>very
</strong>useful.</p>
```

This is what will show in the browser:

```
HTML code is very useful.
```

We will dissect the most important parts of this HTML element:

- **The opening tag:** Contains the element name (here 'p'), wrapped in opening and closing **angle brackets**. This states where that HTML element starts to take effect.
- **The closing tag:** This repeats the element name but preceded this time by a forward slash (/p). This states where the tag's action ceases.
- **The content:** This is the content of the element on which the HTML tags act.
- **Nested tags:** We have shown another HTML element nested between our paragraph tags. It has its own opening tag `<strong>` and closing tag `</strong>`.

1   Type this last HTML example into a text editor (such as Notepad on Windows or TextEdit on Mac. You may need to set the preferences to NOT render text files as HTML). Save it with the name *index.html*, then double click it to open the file again. It should now open in your default web browser and look like the example appearing at the top of this column.
    The original HTML code is called your source code.

2   You can see the source code for any web page element by right clicking on it and choosing 'Select element' or view the entire source code by selecting a 'view source code' menu item usually under the word Developer in your browser. Load any web page and try it.

Common HTML tags

Here are some of the most common tag pairs in HTML with a description of what each one does:

Table 18.1

Common HTML meta tags
`<html>` *html code appears between* `</html>`
`<head>` *defines the header of the page* `</head>`
`<title>` *defines the title of the page* `</title>`
`<body>` *defines the body of the page* `</body>`
`<h1>` *heading* `</h1>`
`<p>` *defines a paragraph* `</p>`
`<b>` *bold* `</b>`
`<i>` *italic* `</i>`
`<div>` *defines a section for applying styles* `</div>`
`<span>` *apply style to text in line with other content* `</span>`

Skill builder: A first HTML page

A typical web page HTML has the following structure. Notice the indenting, which is not essential but makes it easier to see where tags begin and end:

Skill builder

```
<html>
   <head>
       <title>web page title</title>
   </head>
   <body>
       content of web page ...
   </body>
</html>
```

Web pages add other formal elements as well as a heading as shown in the code below.

```
<!DOCTYPE html>
<html>
<head>
<meta charset="utf-8">
<title>My HTML page</title>
</head>
<body>
  <h1>HTML beginnings</h1>
  <p>HTML code is <strong>very
     </strong>useful.</p>
</body>
</html>
```

3 Type out the code as shown in the Skill builder using your text editor. Save it (as *index.html*) and double click it to open in your browser.

Images

As well as pairs of tags, HTML uses some single meta tags for special purposes.

One important one is `img src=` which means 'image source' and allows us to place images on our page from other websites.

We provide the URL of the image inside quotation marks and provide alternative text to display in the browser if the image is not available.

Here is an example:

```
<img src="https://goo.gl/Rphorg"
     alt="Sir Tim Berners-Lee">
```

4 Use your text editor to add this image link code to your *index.html* file, typing it into the body section. Open the index.html file in your browser to view the placed image.

Anchors

The final essential element of HTML is the one that actually makes the World Wide Web operate. It is called an *anchor*.

This special pair of tags provides the ability to cause images or words in a page to link to other pages. These are called *hypermedia* (when linking from text it is called *hypertext*).

It was the concept that Sir Tim Berners-Lee, the inventor of the World Wide Web (but not the Internet), saw as the main purpose of HTML code.

5 First wrap the `<a></a>` tag pair around words you want to be the link. `<a>` stands for *anchor*. Then, add `href=` followed by the URL of the web page we want to link to (`href` stands for **h**ypertext **ref**erence). Type this in the body section of your *index.html* file using your text editor and save it:

```
<a href="https://www.w3.org/People/
   Berners-Lee/Kids.html">Tim
   Berners-Lee explains the web</a>
```

This turns 'Tim Berners-Lee explains the web' into hypertext and links it to the URL inside the quotation marks. The HTML code in your text editor should now look like this:

9780170411820

```
<!DOCTYPE html>
<html>
  <head>
    <meta charset="utf-8">
    <title>My HTML page</title>
  </head>
  <body>
    <h1>HTML beginnings</h1>
    <p>HTML code is <strong>very
      </strong>useful.</p>
    <p>A big thank you to Sir Tim
      Berners-Lee!</p>
    <img src="https://goo.gl/Rphorg"
      alt="Sir Tim Berners-Lee">
    <p><a href="https://www.w3.org/
      People/Berners-Lee/Kids.html">
      Tim Berners-Lee explains the
      web</a></p>
  </body>
</html>
```

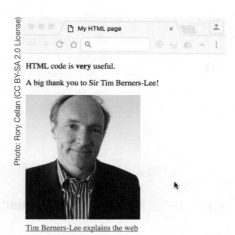

Figure 18.1 The HTML displayed in a browser showing the new hypertext at the bottom

6   Open your *index.html* file in a browser and check it looks like Figure 18.1. Notice the title at the top.
7   Notice the coloured hypertext link now created at the bottom of the web page? Click this link because it is well worth reading Sir Tim Berners-Lee's explanation of how the web works in his own words!

Using Codepen to write your HTML code

Typing in a text editor, saving the file, then opening it again in a browser can be a nuisance. Codepen is a great site for writing, checking and experimenting with HTML code (and other web code we will learn soon in this guided project). You might like to explore the site before you use it. Codepen calls any linked HTML + **Cascading Style Sheets (CSS)** + Javascript code a *pen*. It is really just a web page.

Weblink

8   Some pens on this site are truly amazing. Explore a few of these pens and try them out. Find a simple pen and try changing the CSS to see what happens.
9   When you are ready to start, click the *Create* button to make a new pen and paste the Tim Berners-Lee HTML you have been writing into the left-hand HTML frame. The result will appear in the bottom frame. You can maximise panels by dragging their edges (see Figure 18.2).

Files and folders

When we create a website we need the files to be able to locate one another. Before we go any further, we need to organise all our files inside a single folder we will call *first_web*.

10 Place your index.html page inside this *first_web* folder.
11 You also need a folder to contain *images* and a second for *style* files. Create these now and save them all inside your *first_web* folder.
   - **Images folder**: This folder will contain any images you wish to store locally.

Figure 18.2 Using Codepen for writing, viewing and checking HTML code

- **Styles folder**: This folder is empty now but later will contain code used to add style your web page. We will learn this in the following section.

Your *first_web* folder should now contain these items (Figure 18.3).

index.html   **styles**   **images**

Figure 18.3 When designing a website it is important to organise all your files inside a single folder. Here we see three items forming the contents of a single folder called *first_web*.

Web probe: Learn HTML

This is a good time to learn more HTML. There are many good tutorials on the web but a great place to start is the Mozilla Developer Network. Complete the 'Getting started' and 'HTML' sections now to extend your knowledge of HTML further.

Weblink

CSS

Knowledge probe: CSS

Now that you have learnt HTML essentials you know how to create a simple web page. The first websites used HTML tags to describe the style of text in a web page. These needed to be inserted every time a change in style occurred. Web designers needed another coding language to separate the content (HTML) of the page from its layout style. The method they developed was Cascading Style Sheets or CSS for short. The ability to define styles and reuse them made a huge difference for website designers.

Like HTML, CSS is a description language, not a programming language. CSS is used to change the font, colour, size, background and spacing of your content or to split it into multiple columns.

Here is a snippet of CSS:

```
p {color: purple;}
```

This code would apply a purple colour to all sections of an HTML page that had `<p>  </p>` meta tags.

CSS can be written as part of your HTML file or saved as a separate external file. It is a good habit to write it as a separate file so you can then reuse it.

CSS essentials

A CSS rule is made up of two parts:
- *Selector* states to which elements in your HTML document that rule should apply
- *Properties* describe how content is to appear (e.g. purple text with a border around it).

```
p {color:purple; text-align:center}
```

The above CSS would colour all paragraphs purple and centre them. Note that your CSS code will not work unless 'colour' is spelled 'color'! Note also that it must be placed inside your *styles* folder, as this is part of the path we specified.

Skill builder: A first web page using CSS

Skill builder

1   Create a separate CSS file called *my_styles.css* that contains the following code:

```
h1 {
  color: blue;
  background-color: orange;
  border: 3px solid black;
}
p {
  color: purple;
}
```

2   Place this file inside your *styles* folder and name it *my_styles.css*. The naming must be exact!

3   Add the following code to your HTML file to tell it to link to this CSS external file:

```
<link rel="stylesheet"
  href="styles/my_styles.css">
```

Your HTML should now look like this:

```
<!DOCTYPE html>
<html>
<head>
<meta charset="utf-8">
<title>My HTML page</title>

<link rel="stylesheet" href="styles/
  my_styles.css">
</head>
<body>
<h1>HTML beginnings</h1>
  <p>HTML code is <strong>very
    </strong>useful.</p>
  <p>A big thank you to Sir Tim
    Berners-Lee!</p>
  <img src="https://goo.gl/Rphorg"
    alt="Sir Tim Berners-Lee">
  <p><a href="https://www.w3.org/
    People/Berners-Lee/Kids.html">
    Tim Berners-Lee explains the
    web</a></p>
</body>
</html>
```

Save your changed *index.html* file.

4   Double click it to open in your browser. Does it look like Figure 18.4?

Using Codepen to experiment with your CSS code

5   You should already have used Codepen to create a pen but with only HTML code in the left-hand HTML frame. Now add your CSS code in Codepen's CSS frame. The changed styling for your web page should appear in the bottom frame.

Figure 18.4 Your HTML page with CSS applied. At this stage we are not concerned with how good (or bad!) it looks.

Codepen automatically links to your CSS, but it is good to just leave the link statement in your HTML as it is needed later when your website is in folders (see Figure 18.5).

The box model

CSS uses the idea of nested boxes in deciding how to apply its rules. Each element is imagined as being inside a box, with that box's content, padding, border and margin built up around one another like a big warehouse crate packed with smaller boxes. The outer boxes control styling for the inner boxes. This is why CSS has the word *cascading* in it.

Figure 18.5 Using Codepen for writing, checking and experimenting with HTML and CSS code.

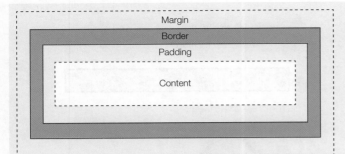

Figure 18.6 CSS uses a box model to decide how to apply its rules.

The box model allows you to add borders around HTML elements and space between them.

- **Content:** The content of the box consisting of text and images.
- **Padding:** The transparent area around content.
- **Border:** The border around both padding and content.
- **Margin:** The transparent area outside the border.

6 Using Codepen with the same HTML code as before, replace the last CSS with the following:

```
body
{
    background-color:antiquewhite;
    height: 450px;
    width: 300px;
    padding: 20px;
    border: 20px solid purple;
    margin: 20px;
}
```

Here the CSS is being applied to the entire *body element* of the HTML. The body element now has a set *width* and *height* with a *padded* transparent area around, a solid purple border 20 pixels wide and a transparent margin around the whole element. The background colour is defined – there are over 100 named colours you can choose from but hex values may also be specified.

The result is shown in Figure 18.7.

Figure 18.7 Adding CSS features

Table 18.2

Common CSS properties and values		
CSS property	**CSS example**	**Explanation**
margin	`margin: 20px`	*Defines space between element border and parent*
padding	`padding: 20px;`	*Defines space between content and border*
border: size style colour	`border: 20px solid purple`	*Select from* `none, dotted, dashed, solid, double`
background-colour	`background-color:antiquewhite`	*Uses colour name or hex value*
font-family	`font-family: "Times New Roman", Times, serif`	Font name in quotes if more than one word. Here if Times New Roman is unavailable will try Times, then will try generic fonts: `sans serif, serif, cursive, fantasy` or `monospace`
font-size	`font-size: 40px`	*Can use pixels (px), ems or percent*
font-style	`font-style: italic`	`none, italic, oblique`
font-weight	`font-weight: bold`	`normal, bold`
text-align	`text-align: center`	`left, right, center, justify`

9780170411820

Common CSS properties and values		
CSS property	**CSS example**	**Explanation**
left, right, top, bottom	`position: relative;` `left: 70px;`	*Sets position but must state absolute or relative first*
height, width	`width: 200px;` `height: 200px;`	*Specifies height and width of an element*
colour	`background-color:purple;` `color:orange`	*Uses colour name or hex value. In this case, a purple background colour and orange text colour*

As the browser renders your code, it works out what styles are to be applied to each box, knowing that if they are contained within other boxes they will take on its rules as well.

7   Use Codepen with the same HTML code as before, and experiment with each of the CSS properties listed in Table 18.2 by altering values. Don't forget to end each with a semicolon!

W3Schools has an easy to read reference with interactive examples for CSS.

Learn CSS

This is a good time to learn more CSS. There are many tutorials on the web but a great place to start is the Mozilla Development Network site.

8   Extend your knowledge of CSS by completing as much of the tutorial as you need.

The best way to learn is to do!

Codepen is a great tool for learning how HTML and CSS work together. It allows you to see immediately the effect of adding and changing CSS code.

9   Try out changing values in your code and experiment changing code for other pens that have been published on Codepen and see what happens.

10 A CSS demo can be found at W3Schools CSS tutorial. Watch as the same HTML code undergoes layout changes when you apply different CSS code – and no CSS code at all.

Class activity: CSS Zen Garden

The CSS Zen Garden demonstrates how the same HTML page can be made to look dramatically different by changing the CSS code.

Weblink

1   Explore the extensive collection of layouts on the site all presenting identical content.
2   Select one favourite from the collection of over 200 and display it on your computer monitor.
3   Each student has three voting counters (such as match sticks) and votes for their three favourites by placing counters at that workstation.
4   Add up the counters.
5   Participate in a class discussion: what made some more popular? (Refer to navigation, readability, consistency, layout, use of white space, audience needs, etc.)

Figure 18.8 Codepen showing Zen Garden code

PROJECT: CSS IN THE GARDEN OF ZEN

The task

Design your own Zen Garden HTML page using CSS.

Planning

1 Plan your design on paper first.

Designing

1 Explore examples on the Zen Garden site to help you generate ideas.
2 Download the HTML file and CSS file provided on the CSS Zen Garden site.
3 Paste these into the appropriate frames in Codepen (see Figure 18.8).
4 Experiment by changing your CSS code.

Implementing

1 Build your final CSS code using your design as your guide (remember you are not to alter the HTML content at all).
2 View the result using various browsers. Are there differences?

_____

_____

_____

_____

Evaluating

1 As earlier, display your final page on your computer. Each student uses three counters (or match sticks) and votes for three favourites by placing counters at those workstations. At the end add up your votes.
2 Discuss in class what made some designs more popular (navigation, readability, consistency, layout, use of white space, audience needs?).

_____

_____

_____

_____

_____

_____

_____

3 What changes would you make if you were to repeat your design?

_____

_____

_____

_____

_____

9780170411820

PROJECT: BUILDING A RELATIONAL FIRST FLEET DATABASE

19

THE TASK

On 24 January 1788, the First Fleet arrived in Botany Bay. The ships had left Portsmouth in England three months before carrying more than 1480 men, women and children onboard.

Your project task is to collect, organise and research data about the convicts of the First Fleet in order to design, build and populate (fill with data) a prototype **relational database** for a future museum display.

Data for this project is available in the online resources on the *Digital Technologies 9 & 10* website.

INFOBIT

Before 1788, Aboriginal peoples had inhabited the world's oldest continent successfully for more than 40000 years. They had seen very few Europeans, but this one event would impact their lives more than any others in their long history.

Between 1788 and 1850 the United Kingdom sent over 162000 convicts to Australia in 806 ships. The first 11 of these ships are today known as the First Fleet and carried the first Europeans (convicts, officials, crew, marines and their families) who settled in the country. Many Australians today are descendants of these convicts and officers.

In Chapter 20 of *Digital Technologies 7 & 8*, you learnt how to build a **flat file database**. In this project you will create a First Fleet relational **database** by linking two separate databases or tables: a convict table and a ship table. Later in Chapter 21 you will use pivot tables and the First Fleet database to quickly extract significant information from the data.

Knowledge probe: Understanding relational databases

A flat **file** database is a single table of data. A relational database is simply one that links separate flat file databases (called tables).

One reason relational databases are important is that they keep data about different types of things together. In a school library database, we would want to separate data about books from data about students and borrowers.

But we also want the tables to have a link of some kind to avoid having to enter the same details twice. For example, if a book was borrowed, we would enter the name of the borrower but not repeat the entry of their details, such as address, email, etc. Unneeded repetition of data in a database is called data **redundancy**, and database designers eliminate all redundant data as far as possible.

The solution is to create a third table called loans, which links the other two (see Figure 19.1).

Knowledge Probe

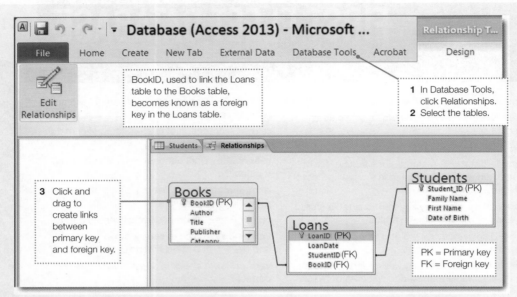

Figure 19.1 A relational database links separate tables. Here a library database links books, loans and student tables.

Relationships

We share many relationships within a family. You will have a biological mother and father but may also have non-biological parents or live with grandparents or another guardian. You may have siblings, cousins, aunts and uncles or very close friends you consider family. You are connected in different ways to each of them.

A relational database is similar, as it maps relationships between things. There are three types of relationships in relational databases:

- One-to-one: for example, a wife has one husband and vice versa. In these cases, you can usually combine both tables into one table without breaking any rules.
- One-to-many/many-to-one: similar to the one between you and a parent. You have only one biological father, but he may have several children. This is true for our First Fleet convict–ships relationship. Each convict can belong to only one ship but each ship can have many convicts.
- Many-to-many: if you have several brothers and sisters, then so do they. Each **record** in both tables can relate

to many records (or no records) in the other table. Many-to-many relationships require a third table, known as a linking table, as in our Library example in Figure 19.1 where the Loans table acts as the linking table.

Linking

Each table in a relational database should have a **primary key** to uniquely identify each entry. This is important as two students may have the same name, or two books the same title. Even Loan table records need this.

When one of these unique primary keys from one table appears in another linked table, it is referred to as a **foreign key** in the second table.

In the library database, book and student primary keys are linked through a third loans table. This is needed as it is a many-to-many relationship: a book can have many borrowers (over time) and a borrower can borrow many books.

Really we are creating a *virtual record* because details in the book table and the student table really only exist in their own tables and are just being mirrored in the loans table so data does not have to be re-entered.

Defining

Note: both MS Access and FileMaker Pro are both suitable tools for building relational databases for this activity.

1 Research the story of the First Fleet using these links, other websites and even library books!

2 The first step in developing any database is to define its purpose. Here we want to be able to search data about convicts who arrived on the First Fleet and data about the ships they arrived on.

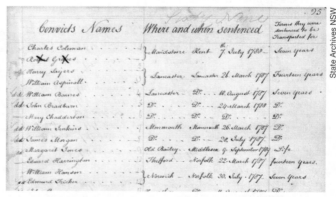

State Archives NSW

Figure 19.2 Original convict record books from which our database was created

9780170411820

Table 19.1 A typical convict record

Number	521
Surname	Owles
Given name	John
Gender	M
Trial date	20/07/85
Place of trial	Surrey
Crime	Aiding escape from prison
Value of crime	0
Sentence	T
Years	7
Trade	No trade
Age	36

Table 19.2

Field	Field type	Validation
Unique ID		
Family name		
Given name		
Age leaving England		
Gender		
Year of death		
Place of trial		
Date of trial		
Crime		
Value of crime (shillings)		
Original sentence		
Transported for (years)		
Occupation		
Ship name		
Notes		

Designing

Data validation and verification

You will not need any actual data until the section 'Creating convict table'. Building a database requires you to plan and design carefully first. When data is entered in a database, it is possible to write rules that check the entered data is at least sensible. This is field **validation**. For example, the year of death for a convict will not be greater than 120 years after the date of arrival of the fleet or before the earliest trial date. A validation rule can be set to ensure that data entered lies between these two values.

A second type of validation is record validation where a record can be checked, say, for two dates to make sure one is always earlier than another. (e.g. here year of trial must precede year of death)

Here's how:
1   Open the table for which you want to validate records.
2   On the Fields tab, in the Field Validation group, click Validation, and then click Record Validation Rule.

A third way to ensure validation when values come from a limited list is to require they be selected from a drop-down menu rather than typed. In Access these are either list boxes or combo boxes. Use online help to find out how to do this.

Verification refers to the accuracy of data. How could you verify the accuracy of the database?

Defining fields

3   Choose suitable **field** types for fields for the convict table, identify a primary field, if possible write a validation rule or if appropriate use a pre-defined list.

4   Choose suitable field types for fields for the ship table, identify a primary field, if possible write a validation rule or if appropriate use a pre-defined list.

Table 19.3

Field	Field type	Validation
Ship name		
Type		
Tonnage		
Master's name		
Number crew		
Number dying on voyage		
Interesting facts		
Image of ship		

5   Design a database layout on paper, carefully positioning naming fields. Imagine your design will end up being used daily, such as in a museum. Consider which fields to feature, font styles and sizes, colour scheme and placement of fields. Do not create your database yet.

Creating Convict table

6 We have provided the convict data online in a number of formats (CSV, tab delimited and Excel spreadsheet). Import as a new table using your database import function (Access can import any of the above formats and all database software can import text or csv files). Alternatively, download a tab delimited file of First Fleet data from the online resources on the *Digital Technologies 9 & 10* website or from the University of Wollongong website.

   If you instead import the data into a existing empty table your database will generate unnamed fields with a sample first record. If so, rename the fields (see Figure 19.3).

7 Define the field types as planned under Designing. Check through the records. Does your import look correct? You should see exactly 780 records.

Creating calculation field

8 You will later need the age at death of the convicts. Add a calculation field to do this. Find out how to create a calculation field in your database application. How will you do this calculation using existing fields? You have fields for Age in 1787 and Year of death.

Creating Ship table

9 Create a new Ship table with fields defined earlier. Enter the data manually using details of the ships provided in the data available on the website Fellowship of First Fleeters. Follow the weblink from the *Digital Technologies 9 & 10* website. This table will have only six entries, as only six out of 11 ships were for convicts.

10 Depending on your database software, the image field holder may be called a name such as Attachment or Container.

Joining tables to create a relational database

11 Use your database software to create a relationship by creating a join between the primary key in the Ship table ('Name') and its matching foreign key in the Convict table (see Figure 19.4).

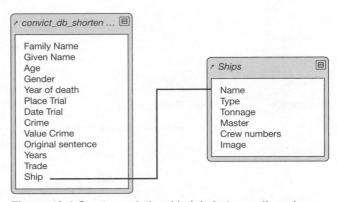

Figure 19.4 Create a relationship join between the primary key in the Ship table ('Name') and its matching foreign key in the Convict table

Creating a layout using the relationship join

12 Your Table style layout for the Convict table will appear similar to Figure 19.5.

   Now create a **form** style layout based on the design completed earlier (see example in Figure 19.6). Position the fields.

What you have created

Because you defined a join relationship on the field 'Ship name' your database application allows you to add fields from the Ships table. Include the image field and data about the ship (see Figure 19.5).

You have now created a relational database where data from a related table is mirrored, using the relationship you defined between the tables. This information could be used to create a database **report**. A report is a customised layout in a database where selected fields are displayed in the form a summary. Report layouts are often designed for printing.

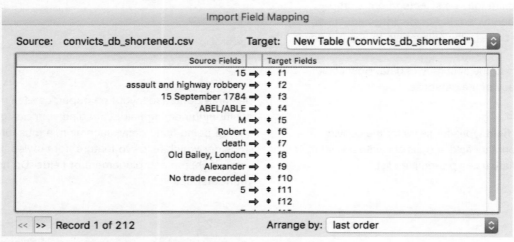

Figure 19.3 Importing the convict data into an empty new table

Family Name	Given Name	Age	Gender	Year of death	Place Trial	Date Trial	Crime
Family Name	Given Name	Age leaving	Gender	Year of Death	Place of Trial	Date of Trial	Crime
		-1 == unknown					
ABEL/ABLE	Robert	15	M		Old Bailey, London	15 September	assault and
ABEL	Mary	30	F	1788	Worcester,	5 March 1785	stealing clothing
ABRAHAMS	Esther	20	F	1846	Old Bailey, London	30 August 1786	stealing lace
ABRAHAMS/ABRA	Henry	28	M		Chelmsford, Essex	9 March 1785	highway robbery
ADAMS	John	47	M	1788(?)	Old Bailey, London	26 May 1784	stealing lead from
ADAMS	Mary	29	F	1788	Old Bailey, London	13 December	stealing clothing
AGNEW/AYNERS	John	27	M		Old Bailey, London	26 May 1784	stealing lead from
AKERS/ACRES	Thomas	29	M	1824	Exeter, Devon	14 March 1785	assault and
ALLEN	Charles	20	M	1794	Old Bailey, London	7 July 1784	stealing linen
ALLEN	John	45	M	1794	Hertford,	3 March 1786	stealing bedding
ALLEN/CONNER	Mary	28	F	1821	Old Bailey, London	10 January 1787	stealing clothing
ALLEN	Mary	22	F	1843	Old Bailey, London	25 October 1786	highway robbery
ALLEN	Susannah	-1	F	1789	Old Bailey, London	18 April 1787	stealing clothing
ALLEN	Tamasin/Jamasin	32	F	1825	Old Bailey, London	25 October 1786	assault and
ALLEN	William	24	M		Ormskirk,	11 April 1785	assault and
ANDERSON	Elizabeth	32	F		Old Bailey, London	10 January 1787	stealing linen
ANDERSON	Frances (Fanny)	30	F		Winchester,	7 March 1786	stealing clothing
ANDERSON	John	26	M		Exeter, Devon	20 March 1786	stealing linen
ANDERSON	John	24	M	1816	Old Bailey, London	26 May 1784	assault and
ARCHER/FORREST	John	31	M	1818	Old Bailey, London	26 May 1784	stealing coach

Figure 19.5 A section of a columnar layout for the First Fleet database.

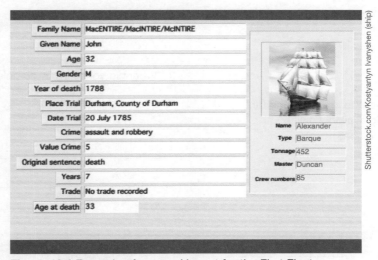

Figure 19.6 Example of a record layout for the First Fleet database. Here ship details are being displayed relationally by linking the Ship table (see blue background) to the Convict table with a one-to-many join.

Implementing

Activity: Using your database for research

The following activities reveal interesting facts about the First Fleet but their main purpose is developing your relational database data analysis and query skills. Your teacher will show you how to perform these queries.

SQL, or Structured Query Language, is a programming language designed to query data from a relational database. The main statement used to query is the SELECT statement. You learn SQL for the project in Chapter 20.

You can answer the following queries, however, without knowing SQL.

Warm-up

Note: The following tasks can be performed using your columnar layout.

First create a document to save your answers in this activity.

1 When was the earliest offence of those on board the First Fleet? (This would have meant that this person had already served seven years of his 99-year term in an English institution before being transported to Australia!)

2 Find out who the oldest and youngest convicts were, and their crimes.

3   Two women, whose trade was 'char woman', were convicted of larceny in 1785. What were their names? Find out what a char woman was.

4   There are lots of Smiths in the fleet. How many Smiths were on board?

5   What was the most common first name for female convicts on the First Fleet? How many were there?

6   How many convicts would have been free settlers after six years in the colony?

Relational

Note: the following tasks can all be performed by searching your relational database using a record layout (with Ship details). You can search by typing the criteria into search fields. Make sure you 'Show all records' before beginning each search.

7   How many convicts sailed on the ship *Alexander*?

8   How many convicts sailed on 'fully rigged ships'?

9   How many convicts sailed on ships over 400 tons?

10 Who was the only apprentice clogmaker and on which ship did they sail?

11 Who was the Master (Captain) of the ship on which convict Humphrey Lynch arrived? How many crew were on board that ship?

The following questions require you to use multiple 'and' finds. Find out how to do this.

12 How many females were on the ship *Alexander*?

13 How many persons less than 20 years of age were convicted of assault?

14 How many persons on board were either butchers or bakers or candlestick makers?

The following task requires a calculation field.

15 You created a calculation field earlier. Remember that you should ignore any age entries listed as –1 as this indicates their ages are not known. How many convicts, as far as we know, died as teenagers?

Evaluating

Compare your database layout to one prepared by the University of Wollongong available online.

Weblink

1   Which interface is easy to use?

_____

_____

_____

_____

_____

_____

2   Which interface is the more useful and why?

_____

_____

_____

_____

_____

_____

3   What did you learn by completing this project?

_____

_____

_____

_____

_____

_____

_____

_____

4   What improvements can you suggest to your project and what would you do differently?

_____

_____

_____

_____

_____

_____

_____

9780170411820

UNDERSTANDING SQL

Those lucky enough to enjoy subscriptions to Netflix, Stan, Quickflix, Foxtel, or other media streaming services may wonder how these services use data to make accurate movie viewing recommendations for customers.

These services collect vast amounts of data in data warehouses, which give them access to detailed movie data, customer data, viewing data, and in some cases their own survey data.

This data would be too much to house in one data table, and would be far too much information for any person to process.

In such cases, data analysts working in these companies make use of *aggregate* or *combined* data solutions and complex algorithms, allowing them to select exactly the specific data they need from their vast data warehouses.

There are many database tools used to manipulate data. Some of the more popular are: Microsoft SQL Server, MySQL, FileMaker and Microsoft Access.

If you do not have access to a database tool, you can engage with one at either Grok Learning or W3schools.

The examples in this section were performed using Microsoft Access, however, you should be able to perform the same functions using your preferred database tool, SQL server, or by using an online database tool at one of the links mentioned above.

THE TASK

In this project you will learn how media streaming companies manipulate the data they collect about you, and you will use SQL (Structured Query Language) to analyse a relational movie database.

The Movies database

Let us imagine we control an online media streaming service. If we think about what data we need to keep within our database, there are some obvious answers.

- We need a data file to hold each of the movies that we have available.
- We also need a data file for each of our customers.
- We need a data file to capture every time one of our customers watches a movie.

Within our sample movies database these three data files have the field captions outlined in Table 20.1.

Table 20.1 Fields within each of the three data files in the Movies database (foreign keys in the View_data file are highlighted).

Movie_data	Customer_data	View_data
Movie_ID	Customer_ID	View_ID
movie_title	Surname	Customer_ID
director_name	First_name	Movie_ID
actor_1_name	DOB	View_date
actor_2_name	Gender	
actor_3_name	City	
genres	State	
duration	Email	
language		
country		
content_rating		
title_year		
budget		
gross		
imdb_score		

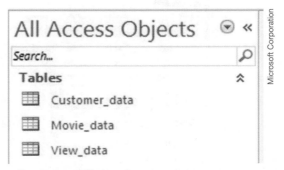

Figure 20.1 Data files as they appear in the Movies database in Access

Each record (row) within each of our data files will contain data from a number of fields (note that the *Movie_data* file has more fields than those shown in Table 20.1).

Because we already have the movie data fields within the *Movie_data* file, and the customer data fields within the *Customer_data* file, we don't need to populate this data again within our *View_data* file, but instead we can link this file to the data within the other two files via the use of *primary* and *foreign* keys (see Chapter 19).

The data for the movies database is sourced from Kaggle Inc. Open Data Commons (ODbL) v1.0.

Download the *SQL_Database* folder from the *Digital Technologies 9 & 10* website and either open the *Movies_DB* Access file or import the three comma separated values (CSV) files using your database tool.

Single file queries

We will begin examining our data by running some simple queries on our *Movie_data* file.

This file houses 29 columns and 2425 rows of data, meaning there are more than 70 000 data items. Using SQL we can break this data into manageable chunks by selecting only the data we require.

Let's start by finding out which of our movies had the biggest budget. To do this we will create a new blank query.

Your database tool will have options for you to create an SQL query for your data. In Access there is a *Query Wizard* and a *Query Design* option.

To conduct data queries using typed SQL code, select the SQL option from the query menus within your database tool. Your teacher will assist you to perform this step with your preferred database tool.

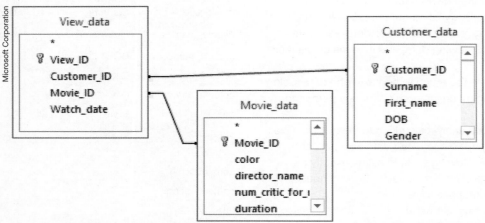

Figure 20.2 Foreign keys in the *View_data* file linked to primary keys in the *Movie_data* and *Customer_data* files

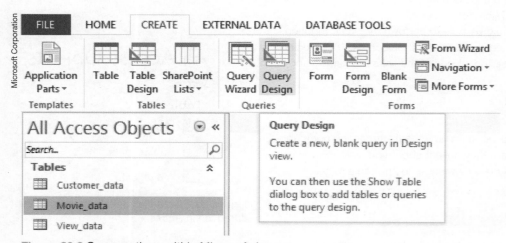

Figure 20.3 Query options within Microsoft Access

9780170411820

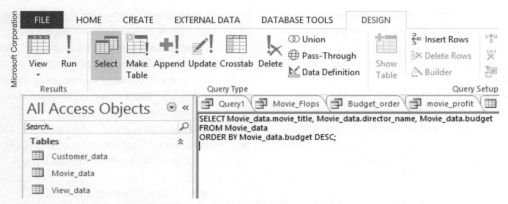

Figure 20.4 The query window and Toolbar options within Microsoft Access

For this query we will need to show at least the *title* and *budget* of each movie, but having the *director's name* would also be handy. If we were to write this query out using plain English, it might look like this:

I want to `select` *movie title*, *director name*, and *budget* `from` *movie data*, and order my data in `descending order` of the *movie budget*.

The SQL for this query code looks very similar to the plain English sentence above:

```
SELECT Movie_data.Movie_title, Movie_
  data.Director_name, Movie_data.
  Budget
FROM Movie_data
ORDER BY Movie_data.Budget DESC;
```

You will notice in our SQL code that the words `SELECT`, `FROM`, `ORDER`, and `DESC` (*descend*) match words in our plain English version. The semicolon at the end of the text signifies that the statement is complete. Also notice that each time one of the fields in our *Movie_data* file is referenced, it is written following the file's name with a full stop like this: `Movie_data.Movie_title`

This is known as dot notation and is sometimes referred to as a membership operator. The full stop here simply identifies the file to which the field belongs.

Type the query into your database tool's query window, save it as *Movie_budget*, and hit *run*.

The query should return the following data to you Figure 20.5.

Knowledge probe: Querying the *Movie_data* file

Continue data analysis on the *Movie_data* file by running the following queries:

1 Show only records where the budget is over 300 million (you can use the keyword `WHERE` and the > operator).
2 Show records where the gross earnings (*Gross*) is above 400 million.
3 Show records where the movie's budget exceeded the gross earnings (movie flops).
4 Return extra fields within these queries such as `Actor_1_name`, `Title_year`, etc.
5 What interesting information did you discover?

Multiple file queries

Now that we have an understanding of how to use SQL to run single file queries, we can begin to access data across multiple files.

movie_title	director_name	budget
Princess Mononoke	Hayao Miyazaki	2400000000
Steamboy	Katsuhiro Ã"tomo	2127519898
Godzilla 2000	Takao Okawara	1000000000
Tango	Carlos Saura	700000000
Pirates of the Caribbean: At World's End	Gore Verbinski	300000000
John Carter	Andrew Stanton	263700000
Tangled	Nathan Greno	260000000
Spider-Man 3	Sam Raimi	258000000
Spider-Man 3	Sam Raimi	258000000

Figure 20.5 Data returned by the *Movie_budget* query

Our *View_data* file contains all of our customers' viewing data. You can imagine how much data this file would house if this were a real movie streaming service!

This file contains the fields: *View_ID*, *Customer_ID*, *Movie_ID*, and *View_date*.

Looking at the raw data within this file provides us with very little insight into the viewing habits of our customers, as it is full of codes. However, if we link the data within this file to the data within our customer and movie files, then we will be able to turn this data into useful information.

View_ID	Customer_II	Movie_ID	View_date
VIEW-0001	ID-0016	MOV-0010	1/01/2016
VIEW-0002	ID-0028	MOV-0090	2/01/2016
VIEW-0003	ID-0008	MOV-0063	3/01/2016
VIEW-0004	ID-0032	MOV-0001	4/01/2016
VIEW-0005	ID-0008	MOV-0025	4/01/2016
VIEW-0006	ID-0025	MOV-0074	6/01/2016
VIEW-0007	ID-0022	MOV-0076	7/01/2016
VIEW-0008	ID-0025	MOV-0063	8/01/2016
VIEW-0009	ID-0004	MOV-0075	9/01/2016
VIEW-0010	ID-0025	MOV-0078	10/01/2016
VIEW-0011	ID-0030	MOV-0081	10/01/2016
VIEW-0012	ID-0019	MOV-0074	10/01/2016

Figure 20.6 Some of the records within the *View_data* file. It is difficult for us to extract information from this table as it consists of codes.

In an SQL database we can use *Joins* to bring in data from other files.

We will join the customer and movie files with our *View_data* file so that we can display the title of the movies rather than just their codes, along with the first name and surname of our customers, rather than just their IDs.

The different joins that can be used are: `INNER JOIN`, `LEFT JOIN`, `RIGHT JOIN`, and `FULL OUTER JOIN`.

You can use any of these joins depending on how you want to bring your data together. To learn more about these joins, search online for 'SQL joins'.

Because we only want to return a list of customer names and movie titles against our *View_data* we will use `INNER JOIN` to link our files together. These links are shown in Figure 20.7.

The SQL code for this looks like this:

```
SELECT View_data.View_ID,Customer_
  data.First_name, Customer_data.
  Surname, Movie_data.Movie_title,
  View_data.View_date
FROM (View_data INNER JOIN Movie_data
  ON View_data.Movie_ID = Movie_data.
  Movie_ID) INNER JOIN Customer_data
  ON View_data.Customer_ID = Customer_
  data.Customer_ID
ORDER BY view_data.View_ID;
```

Here we have told our query to join our *Movie_data* file to our *View_data* file using the *Movie_ID* fieldname, and join our *Customer_data* file to our *View_data* file using the *Customer_ID* fieldname.

Type this code and run it within your database tool to see if it returns a data set the same as Figure 20.8.

Please note that different database systems have their own syntax rules. Here Access requires that the first join statement is placed within parentheses.

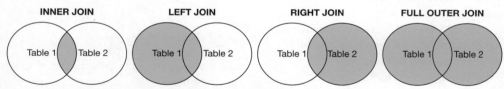

Figure 20.7 The four possible joins that can be used in SQL queries

View_ID	First_name	Surname	Movie_title	View_date
VIEW-0001	Emily	Deng	Batman v Superman: Dawn of Justice	1/01/2016
VIEW-0002	Sofia	Brown	The Polar Express	2/01/2016
VIEW-0003	Ava	Evans	The Legend of Tarzan	3/01/2016
VIEW-0004	Stacey	Nicks	Avatar	4/01/2016
VIEW-0005	Ava	Evans	King Kong	4/01/2016
VIEW-0006	Aiden	Jones	Evan Almighty	6/01/2016
VIEW-0007	Madison	Williams	Waterworld	7/01/2016
VIEW-0008	Aiden	Jones	The Legend of Tarzan	8/01/2016
VIEW-0009	Olivia	Long	Edge of Tomorrow	9/01/2016
VIEW-0010	Aiden	Jones	Inside Out	10/01/2016
VIEW-0011	Evelyn	Davies	Snow White and the Huntsman	10/01/2016
VIEW-0012	Benjamin	Khatri	Evan Almighty	10/01/2016

Figure 20.8 Data returned when the *View_data* file is joined with the *Customer_data* and *Movie_data* files

9780170411820

1 Use the statement `WHERE Movie_data.` `Movie_ID = "MOV-0009";` at the end of your SQL code to find who is watching this movie, and then change the condition to: MOV-0007, MOV-0111, MOV-0838.

2 Find which customers are fans of Johnny Depp. Change the above statement to include *Actor_1_name* instead of *Movie_ID*.

_____

_____

_____

3 How would you find out which customers are fans of Tim Burton movies?

_____

_____

_____

_____

_____

4 Find which customers are the biggest Harry Potter fans. Try using wildcards in you statement like this:

```
WHERE Movie_data.movie_title LIKE
   "Har*";
```

or

```
WHERE Movie_data.movie_title LIKE
   "Har%"
```

Please note that Microsoft Access uses a different character for wildcards than other database tools.

_____

_____

_____

5 It could be useful to know the age of your customers so that you could market specific movies them.

a Use the `DateDiff()` function to find the age of each of the customers in your database by including this statement after `SELECT`. The dateDiff function will return a count for a specific *datepart (in this case years)* between a start date and an end date. In the code below we use the customer's date of birth (DOB) and today's date (Now) to return their age in years. This data gets stored in the field 'Age'.

```
DateDiff("yyyy",Customer_data.
   DOB,Now()) AS Age
```

b Once you have found the age of your customers, use this information to find:

- What is your youngest customer watching? Are there any patterns?

_____

_____

_____

- What is your oldest customer watching? Are there any patterns?

_____

_____

_____

- Which customers would you market the movie MOV-0109 to and why?

_____

_____

_____

- Which customers would you market the movie MOV-1415 to and why?

_____

_____

_____

6 Add some of your classmates to your customer database and design and circulate a survey to gather data to help you recommend and promote movies to these new customers.

7 With your class, discuss the legal and ethical implications associated with data collection methods used by media streaming companies.

8 What did you learn by completing this project?

_____

_____

_____

_____

_____

_____

_____

21

PROJECT: DATA ANALYSIS USING PIVOT POWER!

THE POWER OF THE PIVOT

In a previous project in this section, you were introduced to the database of all convicts sent to Australia by Great Britain on the ships of the First Fleet.

In that project you used a database to answer questions about these convicts.

Another method is using a language called Structured Query Language (SQL) to retrieve data from databases (see Chapter 20). However, it is also possible to manipulate flat file data using a spreadsheet.

In this project you will discover how powerful a spreadsheet's pivot tool can be when analysing flat file data. Again, we will use the data from our First Fleet database.

Imagine you were asked to sort through 780 convict records for the First Fleet and count how many males and females were on each ship. Just a few of these records are shown in Table 21.1. Can you see how tedious and time-consuming this would be? Additionally, it would be very easy to make a small error in counting.

Now imagine being able to answer this question in under 10 seconds!

That, and a lot more besides, is pivot power. The table in Figure 21.1 was created in seconds from a spreadsheet of the 780 convict records.

Many data analysis experts believe pivot tables are the spreadsheet's most powerful feature, yet most users have never used one. Pivot tables produce powerful results and are very fast and easy to use.

Count of Full name	Column Labe ▼		
Row Labels ▼	F	M	Grand Total
Alexander		212	212
Charlotte	20	87	107
Friendship	21	76	97
Lady Penrhyn	102		102
Prince of Wales	50	1	51
Scarborough		211	211
(blank)			
Grand Total	**193**	**587**	**780**

Microsoft Corporation

Figure 21.1 A pivot table of all ships and the numbers of convicts on each was produced in under 10 seconds.

GUIDED PRELIMINARY TASK

For this task, imagine that a history teacher in your school does not know much about spreadsheets, has never heard of pivot tables and has asked for your help using a spreadsheet listing convicts on the First Fleet, the British ships that arrived in Botany Bay on 24 January 1788 with 1480 men, women and children on board.

The teacher needs answers to the following to prepare for class:

* How many convict ships arrived?
* Were some convict ships single-sex only?
* Which gender committed the costliest crimes?
* How many crimes involved as much as the average annual salary? (200 shillings was a rough annual wage for a housemaid or labourer in the 18th century.)
* What crimes were the most common? Does this reveal anything about the society of the time?

1	Full name	Gender	Place of trial	Date of trial	Crime	Value of crime	Sentence	Transported for (years)	Occupation	Convict ship
2	Elizabeth HALL	F	Newcastle	18 January 1786	'Petit' stealing	0.00	Transportation	7	Servant	Lady Penrhyn
3	Charles GRANGER	M	Plymouth	29 December 1786	'Petit' stealing	−1.00	Transportation	7	Leather breeches maker	Friendship
4	Charles McLaughlin	M	Durham	21 July 1785	'Petit' stealing	1.00	Transportation	7	No trade recorded	Alexander
5	John OWLES	M	Croydon	20 July 1785	Aiding a prison escape	0.00	Transportation	7	No trade recorded	Alexander
6	William MURPHY	M	Liverpool	12 January 1786	Assault	0.00	Transportation	7	No trade recorded	Alexander

Table 21.1 A very small section of our 780 convict records as it would look like in Excel.

- What was the average value of the most common crimes?
- Which court tried the most convicts?
- Which court issued the most life sentences?
- Were some courts known to issue more death sentences than transportation sentences (i.e. being sent to Australia)?
- What two occupations were the most common, and which genders dominated these? Does this reveal anything about the society of the time?

You will learn to use pivot tables to answer these by working through an Activity Probe and then complete them via a project.

What is a pivot table?

A pivot table is a summarising tool. It is used to highlight important information from large sets of data simply by dragging chosen field names into its different sections.

It is often much easier to find these answers using pivot tables than using a dedicated database.

Note: All screenshots and instructions in this project are based on the desktop version of Office 365 version of Excel, which is standard across platforms. All activities can be completed using earlier versions of Excel, although locations of items and their appearances will vary.

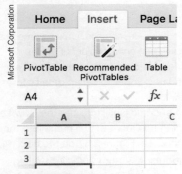

Figure 21.2 PivotTable icon in Excel

Using a pivot table builder

1 Download the spreadsheet provided of convict records (online Pivot Power resources *convict_db_shortened*).
2 Select all the data in your spreadsheet (important!).
3 Select the Insert tab > PivotTable (see Figure 21.2) and accept the range stated.
4 From the pivot table builder section labelled Field Name (see Figure 21.3) you must:
   - drag the field Ship into the Row Labels section
   - drag the field Gender into the Column Labels section
   - drag the field Full name into the Values section.

Figure 21.3 Pivot table builder in Excel with fields at the positions indicated in the activity

Done! What questions can you now answer using this pivot table data?

Notice that the *Full name* field you dragged changed to 'Count of Full name'. Excel assumes this is what we want. The Pivot Builder *counted* how many entries exist for Full name against each Ship, separated into columns by Gender.

You can override this immediately in the Values section drop-down and selecting Count instead by clicking the icon to its right.

5 Add a field to the Report Filter section and discover what this does. Notice a new drop-down menu will appear at the top of your pivot table.

Explore by yourself

Play around with your Pivot Builder a little to get used to it and see if you can answer these historian's questions:
1 How many convict ships arrived? _____
2 Were any convict ships single sex only? _____

A chart or graph based on a pivot table is easy to create in the usual way once you have the pivot table data.

Before reading on, see if you can create the chart shown in Figure 21.4 for the pivot table data above.

Skill builder

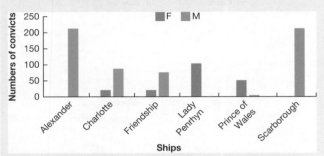

Figure 21.4 Column chart produced from pivot table

1   Using the pivot table data, not the original spreadsheet, Cmd/Ctrl select only the columns with ship names and gender data.
2   From the Insert tab select Insert > Recommended charts > Clustered column.
3   Can you work out how to add the labels to the axes and change legend to M and F as shown in Figure 21.4?
4   Experiment by creating other charts using the convict data.

Doing calculations

You can add calculation columns to your pivot table – it is just like a mini version of your spreadsheet.

1   Set up a new Pivot Builder as shown in Figure 21.5.
    (Note: Do not drag any field into the Columns space as this is generated automatically when Values are used. The word Value here does not refer to our database Value of crime field.)

Figure 21.5 Crimes by gender

Your resulting pivot table should appear like Figure 21.6.

Row Labels	Sum of Value of c	Count of Full name	
F	13669	193	*write formula here*
M	34357.5	587	
Grand Total	**48026.5**	**780**	

Figure 21.6 Pivot table of total value of crimes by gender

You now have the total value in shillings (an amount of money in Britain) listed by gender. Because you included Count of Full name in the Values section of the Builder, you also have numbers of each gender.

2   But this statistic is not fair in judging which gender's crimes were the more expensive, as there were far more males on the fleet than female convicts. Write a simple formula in the empty cell shown on the right of Figure 21.6 to calculate the average value of all the female's crimes. Fill down to find the average value of male crimes.
3   Now can you answer the historian's question. Which gender committed the most costly crimes? _____
4   Repeat steps 1–3 with all Value of crimes amounts converted to their equivalent amounts today by creating an additional column. (200 shillings was a rough annual wage for a housemaid or labourer in the 18th century.)

Grouping data

Next we will try to answer this question: How many crimes had a value greater than the average annual salary of the time?

Grouping is a great feature of pivot tables. Carefully perform these steps and remember to select data before you create pivot tables.

1   Drag the field Value of crime (shillings) into the Row Labels section of the Builder and Count of Full name into the Values section as shown in Figure 21.7 on the next page.
2   Shift-select all amounts less than 200, right-click anywhere in the selection and choose Group and Outline...> Group.
3   Click the symbol next to Group 1 to hide the detail or right-click on the word Group 1 and select > Hide Detail or Click + / − icon shown in the tab PivotTable Tools > Analyse.
4   Shift-select all amounts greater than 200, right-click anywhere in the selection and choose Group and Outline...> Group. Click the disclosure symbol (a + or a triangle) beside the label Group 1 to collapse detail.
5   You can rename the cells 'Group 1' to 'less than annual wage' and Group 2 to 'greater than annual wage'. The result should look like Figure 21.8 on the next page.

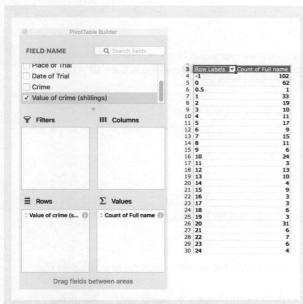

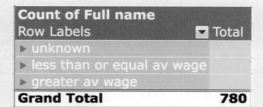

Figure 21.7 Pivot grouping. The section to the right shows all shilling amounts in order down the first column.

Count of Full name

Row Labels	▼ Total
▶ unknown	
▶ less than or equal av wage	
▶ greater av wage	
Grand Total	**780**

Figure 21.8 The table with the results hidden

6 How many crimes were more than an average annual salary? _____

INFOBIT: HANDLING PHONE NUMBERS

There are difficulties in representing phone numbers as numbers as they often contain spaces, brackets and leading zeros. For this reason data analysts use alphanumeric or text for phone numbers. There is no need to store phone numbers as number representations as we don't usually need to perform calculations on them the same way we do with financial or mathematical data.

Skill builder: Cleaning data

Skill builder

Often data needs to be cleaned before using it. This may be because it was originally written by hand in a book or on cards. The clerks who recorded First Fleet data were inconsistent in the way they described crimes and used variant spellings for the same English places. Sometimes cleaning up the data involves making sure it is in the correct format. Dates have been handwritten using different formats over the years.

Before the original First Fleet database could be used for this book, its data needed a lot of 'cleaning up'. We have collected some of these issues in this table.

For each issue, complete the table describing how it could be fixed and how you believe this would have affected the use of the data if not fixed.

This wordbank will give you hints to help fill in the method column:

serial number, replace term, drop-down menu, strip white space, additional column, convert with formula

Table 21.2

Data clean-up issue	Method to fix	Effect if not fixed
In the field for the Trial place names, many entries had alternative spellings for the same place.		
Many convicts had the same name.		
Some entries had two places of Trial for the one person as the convict had been tried twice.		
Sometimes entries for Gender had spaces after them.		
(Not fixed) When the value of a crime was not known it is recorded as –1.		
(Not fixed) Most spreadsheets cannot represent dates before 1900.		

THE TASK

Defining

Your task is to answer the historian's remaining questions:

- What crimes were the most common? Does this reveal anything about the society of the time?
- What was the average value of the most common crimes?
- Which court tried the most convicts?
- Which court issued the most life sentences? (Note: To sort on a column in a PivotTable, right-click on any value in the column and select Sort).
- Were some courts known to issue more death sentences than transportation sentences (i.e. being sent to Australia)? This requires use of the Filter box in Excel's PivotTable Builder.
- What two occupations were the most common and which genders dominated these? Does this reveal anything about the society of the time?

Designing

Determine the fields needed to answer each query by completing this table. Add two research questions of your own.

Table 21.3

Research question	Fields needed to build pivot table
What crimes were the most common?	
What was the average value of the most common crimes?	
Which court tried the most convicts?	
Which court issued the most life sentences?	
Were some courts known to issue more death sentences than transportation sentences (i.e. being sent to Australia)?	
What two occupations were the most common and which genders dominated these?	

Implementing

Taking each question in turn, use the Pivot Builder in your spreadsheet application to produce a pivot table and record the result for each in this table.

Table 21.4

Research question	Research results
What crimes were the most common?	
What was the average value of the most common crimes?	
Which court tried the most convicts?	

Research question	Research results
Which court issued the most life sentences?	
Were some courts known to issue more death sentences than transportation sentences (i.e. being sent to Australia)?	
What two occupations were the most common and which genders dominated these?	

Evaluating

1 Ask a history teacher to visit your class and select a number of students to demonstrate pivot tables and briefly present the results of the project.
2 Next, ask the teacher if they would like to comment on the usefulness of these results from an historian's point of view.
3 Ask the history teacher to share with the class what life was like in the colony following the arrival of the Fleet and the interactions between colonists, convicts and local Aboriginal people.
4 Summarise the history teacher's remarks.

_____

_____

_____

_____

_____

_____

_____

_____

_____

_____

_____

_____

Challenge!

1 See if you can fix the pre-1900 dates spreadsheet problem in the original First Fleet spreadsheet.
2 Create an additional column in your First Fleet database that has all the trial dates in the form YYYYMMDD to allow chronological sorting.

22

PROJECT: ANALYSING AND VISUALISING BIG DATA

big data Very large structured or unstructured data sets that can be analysed to reveal patterns or trends, especially relating to human behaviour, such as the set of all Google search terms for one year

data analysis The process of transforming and modelling data with the aim of discovering useful information

THE TASK

Your task in this project is to use three very different big **data analysis** tools and evaluate their usefulness.

Figure 22.1

Tool 1: Google Trends

Using Google Trends

Weblink

Google Trends shows currently trending search terms and can be used to track the popularity of terms used in Google searches over time. It is a powerful online tool as it gives free and open access to data from the most used search tool on the planet! You can also compare more than one search term at once. Locate the tool by searching the Internet for 'Google Trends' (see Figure 22.2).

Web probe: *Year In Search*

Each year Google creates a short video called *Year In Search 20XX* (where 20XX is the year) based on the most popular items searched by Google users in that year.

Video

View two of these videos – the most recent and an earlier year. Is there a central message in each?

_____

_____

_____

_____

_____

_____

_____

_____

_____

_____

_____

_____

_____

9780170411820

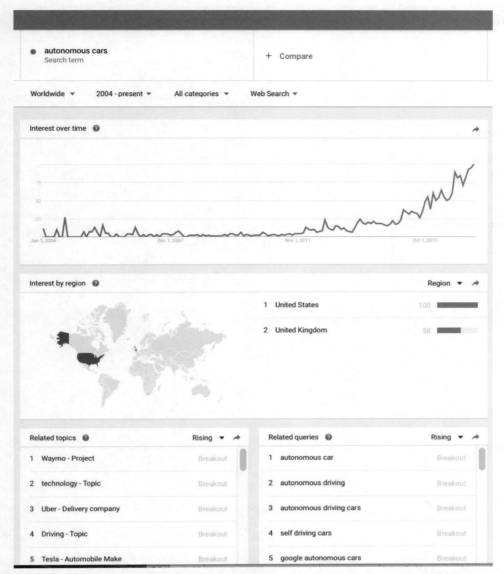

Figure 22.2 Google Trends shows terms used in Google searches over time along as well as mapping geographical trends. This search shows the growth of interest in autonomous cars.

1 Your task is to complete this table using Google Trends and the 2004–present setting. Add two trend terms of your own.

Table 22.1

Google Trends terms	Your interpretation of the Google Trends graph
Shot put	
Refugee	

Google Trends terms	Your interpretation of the Google Trends graph
Syria	
Malcolm Turnbull, Kevin Rudd (separate items)	
iPhone, Android (separate items)	
Your own research	

2   List the Google Trends topics trending in Australia today and explain why you think they are trending.

Table 22.2

Weblink

Trending now	Why?

9780170411820

1 Discuss what use the following groups might have for the Google Trends tool:
   • advertisers
   • politicians
   • school students
   • media.
2 Discuss whether data trends are open to misinterpretation.
3 Record your conclusions.

_____

_____

_____

_____

_____

_____

_____

_____

Tool 2: Google Ngrams

Weblink

Google Ngram Viewer (Figure 22.3) graphs all words found in the 25 million books scanned by Google so far. It is estimated the world has around 130 million books (of which this is one!).

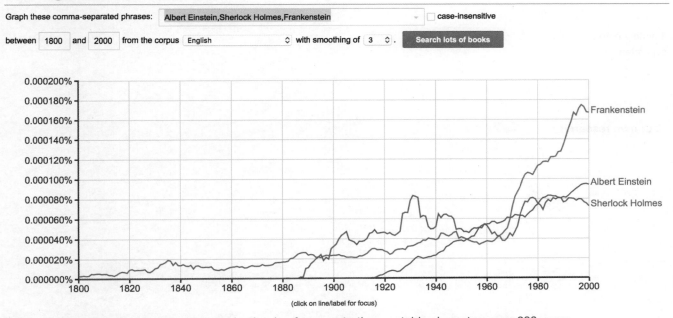

Figure 22.3 Google's Ngram viewer comparing book references to three notable characters over 200 years

1 Locate Google's Ngram Viewer online and complete this table using it.

Table 22.3

Term to type in Google Ngram Viewer	Your explanation
Atomic	
Love, hate (comma separated items)	
Bathroom, toilet, dunny, restroom, powder room	
Wii, PlayStation, Xbox	
Refugee	
iPhone, Android (comma separated items)	
Your own research	

9780170411820

2 Use Google Trends with the two search terms 'iPhone' and 'Android'. Next, use Google Ngrams to track the same two terms (separated by a comma). We get very different results. Why?

_____

_____

_____

_____

Tool 3: Visualising data with Gapminder

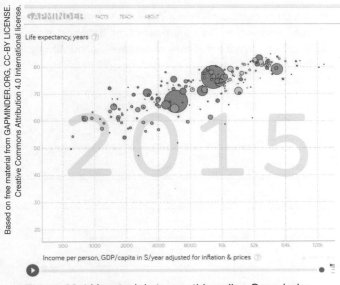

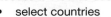
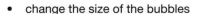
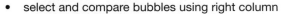

Figure 22.4 Your task is to use this online Gapminder bubble graph tool to analyse global big data.

Using a visual data analysis tool

A large amount of research involves detecting trends in very large amounts of data. Data scientists have developed many different ways to visualise data. Your task is to use the online Gapminder bubble graph tool to analyse global **big data**.

Web probe: *200 Years That Changed the World*

1 Watch the Hans Rosling video *200 Years That Changed the World*. It will help you learn to use the Gapminder tool.

2 Summarise the content of his video.

_____

_____

_____

_____

_____

_____

_____

_____

_____

1 Visit the Gapminder website, where you can access a 'How to use' button to:
- select countries
- change the size of the bubbles
- select and compare bubbles using right column
- drag time slider
- zoom
- turn trails on/off for individual countries

When you have done this you might like to switch to the newer version or download a desktop version of Gapminder by searching for 'Gapminder offline version'.

Gapminder graphs five things at once: the two axes (such as income and life expectancy), size of the bubble (population), region (colour) and time (play button).

2 Now set up and run these enquiries:
- Is there a relationship between income and the children per woman? Is Australia typical?
- Investigate life expectancy versus children per woman.
- The Bangladesh miracle: Child mortality against Children per woman.

3 Summarise your discoveries.

_____

_____

_____

_____

_____

4 Why do you think big data has emerged as a concern recently?

_____

_____

_____

_____

_____

5 Use the site Global Rich List at home, with the help of an adult, to find how rich your family is compared to the world. You might be surprised!

Evaluating

1 For each database state how the data was collected.

Weblink

_____

_____

_____

_____

_____

2 How accurate do you believe the data is for the data used by each of these tools?

_____

_____

_____

_____

3 All three tools used visual elements to communicate data trends. How effective were each of these compared to presentation of the same data in the form of a table?

_____

_____

_____

_____

4 Do you think any of the tools limited your access to the data?

_____

_____

_____

_____

5 Did any of the tools allow access and storage of data?

_____

_____

_____

_____

6 Do any issues of privacy or security arise for these databases tools?

_____

_____

_____

_____

7 Research or class discussion: What are the major issues for society today as a result of big data and data aggregation? What responses should we, as individuals, make?

_____

_____

_____

_____

_____

_____

_____

_____

_____

9780170411820

Figure 23.1 The Worx Landroid autonomous lawn mowing robot

THE TASK

In this project you will be given the opportunity to build your own autonomous robot.

This project can be as challenging as you wish. In Project 5 you build a complete autonomous robot on your own, using the sub-systems you have created in Projects 1–4. Project 5 demands a great deal of accuracy and will test you. If you just want to learn about the various sub-systems and how they work, then limit yourself to Projects 1–4 only.

The projects in this chapter can be done individually or in groups of two to four.

DIGITAL EMBEDDED SYSTEMS IN AN ANALOG WORLD

You may have been caught up in the recent drone and robot craze that has swept the globe. Larger versions of these are set to change the way we live our lives, from how we receive our mail to how we receive takeaway food. Unmanned (autonomous) vehicles are now being used for everything from carrying lifesaving defibrillators to delivering pizza.

Web probe: Unmanned vehicles

Google these acronyms to learn more about unmanned vehicles: UGV, UAV, USV, UUV.

These vehicles would not be possible without digital technologies; however, even though these embedded systems are digital devices, they still have to interact with an analog world. The way that these devices interact with the real world is via their sensors and actuators.

We have already learnt in *Digital Technologies 7 & 8* how digital systems deal with defined or finite sets of values, whereas analog data is represented by smooth and continuous values. One form of analog data can be represented as a sine wave, whereas digital data would need to be represented as a square wave (Figure 23.2).

Sine   Square

Figure 23.2 Sine wave (left); square wave (right)

In order for our embedded digital systems to interact with the analog world, they must have a way of converting analog data to digital and digital data to analog.

The micro-controllers in these embedded digital systems have what is known as analog-to-digital-converters (ADC), which allow them to convert the analog input voltage data from sensors into digital data.

They also have a system called **pulse width modulation (PWM)**, which allow them to simulate analog data that can be used to control outputs, such as the speed of a motor or the dimming of a light.

Modern autonomous vehicles have a number of analog sensors that allow them to know their position with reference to their surroundings. Examples are:

- An accelerometer – which measures acceleration and change in velocity.

- A magnetometer – which measures the magnetic fields of the Earth like a compass.

The analog actuators on these vehicles include:

- Brushed and brushless motors: Continuous drive – used for movement.
- Servo motors: Precise position – used for steering or changing direction.

Skill builder: Guided project 1

Changing the speed of a DC motor

Skill builder

This project builds upon the learning in *Digital Technologies 7 & 8*, and will help you understand how digital systems drive motors with a simulated analog (PWM) output, and give you an appreciation of how serial communication can be used for both communication and debugging.

Materials

Weblink

- Arduino Uno board (or equivalent) and USB cable (if you do not have an Arduino Uno, you can complete this project using an online emulator)
- the Arduino IDE and drivers loaded onto a computer
- project code provided in the online resources on the *Digital Technologies 9 & 10* website downloaded to a folder on your computer called *Autonomous Robot Project*
- 1 breadboard
- 1 2N222 NPN type transistor (or equivalent)
- 1 small DC motor with a fan blade attached (6 to 12 volt)
- a 1KΩ resistor
- a 1N4001 diode (or equivalent)
- a 0.1 µF capacitor (or equivalent)
- 5 pin-to-pin breadboard jumper wires
- a 6 × AA battery pack (9 volt)

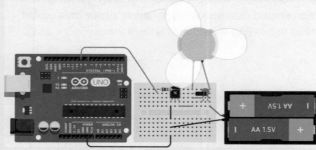

Figure 23.3 The circuit layout for the *motorFan* sketch. Go to the *Digital Technologies 9 & 10* website to view a larger version. Refer also to the circuit diagram in Figures 23.7 and 23.8.

From within the Arduino IDE, open the *motorFan* sketch from your *Autonomous Robot Project* folder. Study this sketch by noticing the code at the top of the sketch, within the SETUP, and within the LOOP. Try to predict what the layout in Figure 23.3 will do when run with this sketch.

Parts of the sketch

1 The system waits for the input of a character from a specific set.
2 Upon receiving one of these characters it converts this data to data that drives the DC motor.
3 It prints a message to the serial monitor (the motor's speed or an error message).

The key pieces of code

1 `int motorPin = 9;`

   Declare and define the *motorPin* variable attached to pin 9 on the Arduino. On the Arduino Uno there are only 6 pins that can be used for PWM (pins 3, 5, 6, 9, 10, 11).

2 `Serial.begin(9600);`
   `Serial.println("Please enter a number between 0 and 9 to change the motor");`

   Start Serial communication and print the opening message.

3 `if ( Serial.available()) {`
   `char ch = Serial.read();`
   `if(ch >= '0' && ch <= '9') // is ch a number between 0 and 9?`
   `{`
   `int revSpeed = map(ch, '0', '9', 0, 255);`
   `analogWrite(motorPin, revSpeed);`

   Wait for the input of a character between 0 and 9.

   Convert this to a number between 0 and 255, and analogWrite this to the motor. The analogWrite function sends the PWM pulse to the motorPin.

4 `Serial.print("Unexpected character ");`

   The system will also print an error message if a character outside of the range is entered.

9780170411820

Build and test the sketch

1 Build the *motorFan* circuit as shown in Figure 23.3.

2 Upload the sketch to your Arduino board.

3 Open the serial monitor, which should greet you with an opening message.

4 Entering a character between 0 and 9 on your keyboard should set your motor running at the appropriate speed, and you should see a message indicating the motor's speed printed to the serial monitor.

5 If your system is not working as expected, you will need to *debug* your circuit and code.

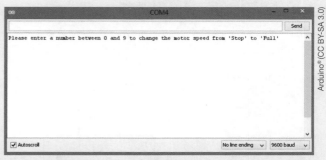

Figure 23.5 The serial monitor window in the Arduino IDE

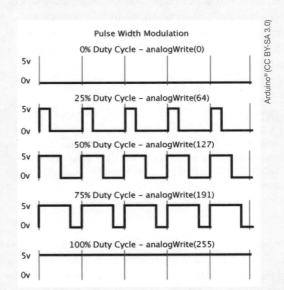

Figure 23.4 The serial monitor can be accessed under the Tools menu

Using debug code

If your system doesn't work, how do you know if the bug is in the code or the circuit?

The use of debug code placed throughout your sketch provides you with a printed output that should match the physical outputs produced by your system.

In our *motorFan* sketch we have included code that prints the motor's speed to the serial monitor. By entering a '9', the motor should run at full speed and the message 'The speed of the motor is 255' will be printed. If you get this message but the motor is not running, then you know that the bug must be in your circuit.

Knowledge probe: How this sketch works

When the system receives an appropriate character as an input it uses the *map* function to convert this data into a number between 0 and 255 (known as the *duty cycle*). This number determines the width of the pulse, which outputs to the *motorPin*, increasing the voltage with the number value (Figure 23.6).

Our circuit has been set up with two independent power supplies (5 volts from the Arduino and 9 volts from the battery pack), and we have used a *transistor* in our circuit to act as a switch. This means that when 5 volts is applied to the base leg of our transistor via the *motorPin* (pin 9), it allows the current to flow from the 9 volt battery pack, and this drives the motor. As well as controlling the amount of voltage and current flowing through the circuit, this setup allows you to amplify the voltage from our Arduino's 5 volts to the 9 volts supplied from the battery pack or even greater.

The 5 volts supplied by the Arduino is called the *logic voltage*, and the 9 volts from the battery is called the *power voltage*.

The small *capacitor* in *parallel* with the motors helps to absorb electrical noise generated by the motor, and the *diode* helps to protect the circuit's components from left over electrical energy when the motor is switched off. This is one of the fundamental circuits in moving digital systems.

Figure 23.6 The PWM duty cycle – from no pulse (0 volts) to a full pulse (5 volts)

How do these components work: DC motor, NPN and PNP transistors, diode, capacitor?

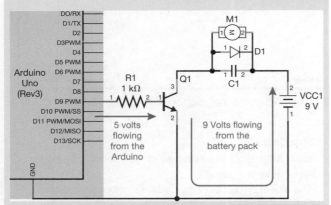

Figure 23.7 Motor circuit with 5 volt logic and 9 volt power (showing conventional current flow).

PROJECT 2

Adding an ultrasonic sensor

The previous project allowed you to see how PWM works to drive a motor, and how serial communication can be used to send commands and help to debug a system.

The *motorFan* sketch relied on manual inputs to control the fan (an open loop system), so in this project we will replace this manual control with automated control (closed loop system). To do this we will use an ultrasonic range finder.

INFOBIT

There are a number of ultrasonic range finders available for use. Some have 3 pins and some have 4 pins like the HC-SR04. Code for both 3 pin and 4 pin devices have been included in this chapter.

The ultrasonic range finder is a digital sensor that sends a digital signal in the form of an ultrasonic 'ping', and receives this signal back as an echo. The Arduino micro-controller calculates the time difference between the send (*trig*) and receive (*echo*) signals to work out the distance of an object in front of the sensor. This system allows digital data in the form of the 'ping' to be converted into data that accurately measures the analog movement of an object (or movement toward an object).

In this project we create a system that switches a fan ON when it detects an object within 1 metre, and decreases the fan's speed as the object gets closer.

To do this we need to test two conditions, min and max distance, and have some way of converting this data into data that can control the fan's speed.

Here is the algorithm in structured English:

```
SensorFan
WHILE
  Read echoPin
  Covert echoPin data to cm
    IF cm > 5 and cm < 100
      Convert cm from range 5-100 to
        range 50-255
      Send this data to motorPin in
        PWM pulse
    ELSE
      Send a 0 pulse to motorPin
    ENDIF
ENDWHILE
EXIT
```

Materials

- All of the resources from the previous project
- An ultrasonic range finder (either 3 pin or 4 pin) with plastic holder

Build and test the sketch

1   Open the *sensorFan* sketch from your *Autonomous Robot Project* folder.
2   Study this sketch and locate the code that resembles the structured English above.
3   This sketch has a small bug in the code that will cause the system to function incorrectly. Locate this bug and correct it (hint: check operators within control structures).
4   Set up your circuit the same as the circuit in Figure 23.8. If you are using a 3 pin sensor, attach the SIG pin to pin A0 on your Arduino, or if using a 4 pin sensor, attach the Trig pin to pin A0 and the Echo pin to pin A1 on your Arduino.
5   The other two pins should be connected to GND and +5V.

This sketch contains two functions that have been written for the ultrasonic range finder (one for the 3 pin sensor and one for the 4 pin sensor). Can you locate these functions within the *sensorFan* sketch?

There are two lines of code inside the loop function of this sketch that call these functions. These are:

```
cm = Ping3Pin(trigPin);// comment
  out this line if using a 4 pin
  sensor
cm = Ping4Pin(trigPin, echoPin);//
  comment out this line if using a 3
  pin sensor,
```

Remember that commenting out code makes this code invisible to the micro-controller. To comment out this code,

9780170411820

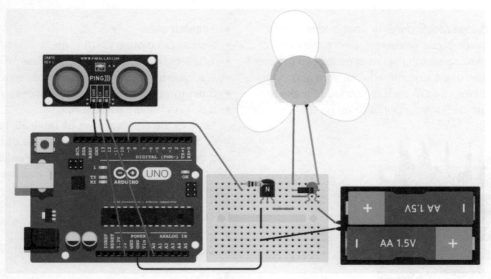

Figure 23.8 Circuit setup for the *sensorFan* sketch, using an ultrasonic range finder

simply place two forward slashes at the start of the line like this:

```
//cm = Ping3Pin(trigPin);// comment
    out this line if using a 4 pin sensor
```

You need to comment out whichever of these two lines does not apply to your sensor.

Change the code in your sketch to match your ultrasonic sensor, then upload the code and test your system by placing your hand or an object in front of the sensor.

You should observe that the fan only runs when you have an object within 1 metre of the sensor. The fan should be on full when your object is approximately 1 metre from the sensor, and the fan's speed should decrease to about 1/5 the speed as your object approaches the 5 cm mark.

If your system did not function as expected, you will need to check that you picked up the bug previously mentioned (check the greater than and less than operators), and also check for bugs in your circuit.

Knowledge probe: How this sketch works

Knowledge Probe

If you study the code within the *Pin4Pin* function, you will see that the trig pin (trigger) is initially set LOW and then driven HIGH to send a pulse for 5 microseconds. Then the trig pin is switched LOW and the echo pin switched HIGH to read the pulse echo:

```
pulseIn(echo, HIGH);
```

This data is stored in the variable *pingTime* and then converted to a distance in centimetres using the equation: *(pingTime / 29) / 2*

Sound in air takes approximately 29 microseconds to travel 1 cm, which means it takes 2900 microseconds to travel 1 metre. There are 1 million microseconds in one second, which means that it takes 0.0029 seconds to travel 1 metre, which is approximately 345 metres per second (speed of sound = 343 m/s).

1 Can you work out why we also divide this result by 2?

_____

_____

_____

2 What would the distance of the object be if the ping took 500 microseconds to return?

_____

_____

_____

INFOBIT

Recently a system very similar sensor to this has been deployed in large car parks to indicate available car spaces with a green light.

The ultrasonic range finder sends out an ultrasonic sound pulse that is audible to dogs and cats. This device is sometimes used in systems designed to stop dogs from barking.

PROJECT 3

Changing the direction of two DC motors with L298N

So far we have been able to simulate analog output to drive our motor, and read and process analog inputs using a digital sensor; however, we are yet to create a system that would move a robot.

In this project we will be using a special module attached to our Arduino that will allow us to control both the speed and direction of two DC motors, which means that we can have full control over a robot's movement.

The *L298N H-Bridge Motor driver* is what is known as a *Dual Full Bridge Driver*. It can be used to switch the current in a circuit ON as well as switch the direction for two motors, meaning that we can use it to control the forward and reverse direction of the two DC motors needed to make a robot move *forward*, *backward*, *right*, and *left*.

Motor 1

Motor 2

Remove jumpers for PWM from Arduino

Vin, GND, +5V out   ENA, IN1, IN2, IN3, IN4, ENB

Figure 23.9 The L298N Dual H-Bridge Motor Driver module

The H-Bridge works like a series of switches or gates and its circuit is structured in an H shape. The L298N module has two H-Bridges.

By opening two of the switches and closing the other two, you can change the flow of current from one direction to the opposite (Table 23.1).

Coding, building, and testing the Dual_motor sketch

Materials

- Arduino Uno board (or equivalent) and USB cable
- the Arduino IDE and drivers loaded onto a computer
- project code provided in the online resources on the *Digital Technologies 9 & 10* website downloaded to a folder called *Autonomous Robot Project* on your computer

- 1 breadboard
- 2 small DC motors (6–12 volt)
- 1 L298N Dual H-Bridge motor driver module
- 6 socket-to-pin breadboard jumper wires
- 3 pin-to-pin breadboard jumper wires
- a 6 × AA battery pack (9 volt).

Look at the first few rows of Table 23.1 and study what the code is doing relative to the image of the H-Bridges and the motors' direction. Fill in the blanks to complete the code for each of the functions that are needed for the Dual_motor sketch.

Motor 1

- in1 controls switch S1 and S4
- in2 controls switch S2 and S3.

Motor 2

- in3 controls switch S1 and S4
- in4 controls switch S2 and S3.

The 'in' pins control the direction, and the 'en' pins control the speed (see Table 23.1).

Open the *Dual_motor* sketch from your *Autonomous Robot Project* folder and copy your solution from the table above into the appropriate functions. The goForward function has been done for you.

Build the *Dual_motor* circuit by carefully replicating the circuit illustrated in Figure 23.10. Use the socket-to-pin jumper wires to connect the EN and IN pins on the L298N module to your Arduino board.

Once you have completed the code and built the circuit you can upload the sketch to your Arduino and test your system.

Opening the serial monitor you will be greeted with the message: `"type: 'w' forward, 's' back, 'a' left, 'd' right, 'x' stop"`.

If you enter in one of these commands you should get the appropriate response from your motors.

If you notice that one of your motors is moving in the opposite direction than it should, simply swap over the wire connections for this motor to the L298N module.

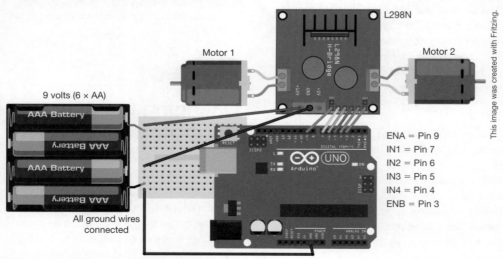

9 volts (6 × AA)

All ground wires connected

L298N

Motor 1

Motor 2

ENA = Pin 9
IN1 = Pin 7
IN2 = Pin 6
IN3 = Pin 5
IN4 = Pin 4
ENB = Pin 3

This image was created with Fritzing.

Figure 23.10 Circuit for the Dual_motor sketch, using the L298N module

9780170411820

Table 23.1 H-Bridge and code configuration for two motors; motor 2 should be wired opposite to motor 1 because it will be on the opposite side of the robot

Direction	Code	Motor 1	Motor 2

Off	```void allOff()```
	 ```{```
	 ``` digitalWrite(in1, LOW);```
	 ``` digitalWrite(in2, LOW);```
	 ``` digitalWrite(in3, LOW);```
	 ``` digitalWrite(in4, LOW);```
	 ```}```		

Forward	```void goForward()```
	 ```{```
	 ``` digitalWrite(in1, HIGH);```
	 ``` digitalWrite(in2, LOW);```
	 ``` analogWrite(enA, 255);```
	 ``` digitalWrite(in3, HIGH);```
	 ``` digitalWrite(in4, LOW);```
	 ``` analogWrite(enB, 255);```
	 ```}```		

Backward	```void goBackward()```
	 ```{```
	 ``` digitalWrite(in1,);```
	 ``` digitalWrite(in2,);```
	 ``` analogWrite(enA, 200);```
	 ``` digitalWrite(in3,);```
	 ``` digitalWrite(in4,);```
	 ``` analogWrite(enB, 200);```
	 ```}```		

Right	```void goRight()```
	 ```{```
	 ``` digitalWrite(in1,);```
	 ``` digitalWrite(in2,);```
	 ``` analogWrite(enA, 200);```
	 ``` digitalWrite(in3,);```
	 ``` digitalWrite(in4,);```
	 ``` analogWrite(enB, 200);```
	 ```}```		

Left	```void goLeft()```
	 ```{```
	 ``` digitalWrite(in1,);```
	 ``` digitalWrite(in2,);```
	 ``` analogWrite(enA, 200);```
	 ``` digitalWrite(in3,);```
	 ``` digitalWrite(in4,);```
	 ``` analogWrite(enB, 200);```
	 ```}```		

PROJECT 4

Writing a class for our motor module

Take another look over the Dual_motor sketch and notice how much code this sketch contains.

There are five different function definitions, not including the standard SETUP and LOOP functions, as well as definitions for the variables and commands.

With so much code the sketch becomes messy and difficult to read. In these situations code can become mixed up and mistakes can easily be made. Programmers use structures called *classes* and *libraries* to contain parts of the code. By making use of these classes and libraries, certain parts of the code can be hidden away. This makes the program easier to follow as there is less detail, and it protects that code from alteration. We call the process of hiding parts of the code away *abstraction*.

We have learnt already that abstraction is part of computational thinking but it is also part of Object Oriented Programming (OOP), and that this process of encapsulation helps to protect these code parts within containers.

In this project we will take all the specialised functions from our Dual_motor sketch and place them inside a class and library, so that this code can be easily used by others. The use of classes means that we have now started to program in OOP. You learnt about OOP if you completed the project in Chapter 10. You will see how this works when we start programming our board.

We will call our library H-Bridge, and will need to create two separate files to contain our new library: *Hbridge.h* (header file, which contains the library definition, and class definition with function and variable declarations), and *Hbridge.cpp* (source file, which contains the function definitions).

You will not be able to write these files inside the Arduino IDE, but you can use any plain text editor or source code editor such as: Notepad (Windows), TextEdit (Mac).

From your *Autonomous Robot Project* folder open the *Hbridge.h* and *Hbridge.cpp* files with your plain text editor and observe the code (do not make changes at this point).

There are some programming conventions that must be followed to make these files work correctly. These will be briefly explained as we work our way through, but don't worry too much at this stage if you don't fully understand these conventions.

We will start with the Hbridge.h file.

Creating the header file

The body of code in this file consists mainly of all of our function statements and variables contained within a class.

At the top of the header file we have included the statement to bring in all of the code from the Arduino standard library `#include "Arduino.h"`.

We need to place the body of our code within a few lines of code that ensure that nothing goes wrong if someone accidentally includes our library twice.

```
#ifndef Hbridge_h
#define Hbridge_h
// your code goes here
#endif
```

The complete code can be viewed in Figure 23.12.

Creating the source file

The source file *Hbridge.cpp* requires both the Arduino standard library and our own *Hbridge.h* library to be included at the top.

```
#include "Arduino.h"
#include "Hbridge.h"
```

Next we have created a **constructor**, which will tell the program what to do when someone creates a new object with our library. This constructor defines all of the pins we need to make our motors run (see Figure 23.13).

```
11    class Hbridge
12    {
13      public:
14        Hbridge(int in1, int in2, int in3, int in4, int enA, int enB);
15        void allOff();
16        void goForward();
17        void goBackward();
18        void goRight();
19        void goLeft();
20      private:
21        int _in1;
22        int _in2;
23        int _in3;
24        int _in4;
25        int _enA;
26        int _enB;
27    };
```

Public members - Can be used by all parts of the program

Private members - can only be used within the class

Figure 23.11 The class definition inside the H-bridge library header file

9780170411820

```
 6    #ifndef Hbridge_h
 7    #define Hbridge_h
 8
 9    #include "Arduino.h"
10
11    class Hbridge
12    {
13      public:
14        Hbridge(int in1, int in2, int in3, int in4, int enA, int enB);
15        void allOff();
16        void goForward();
17        void goBackward();
18        void goRight();
19        void goLeft();
20      private:
21        int _in1;
22        int _in2;
23        int _in3;
24        int _in4;
25        int _enA;
26        int _enB;
27    };
28    #endif
```

Figure 23.12 Code within the H-bridge library header file

```
10    Hbridge::Hbridge(int in1, int in2, int in3, int in4, int enA, int enB)
11    {
12      pinMode(in1, OUTPUT);
13      pinMode(in2, OUTPUT);
14      pinMode(in3, OUTPUT);
15      pinMode(in4, OUTPUT);
16      pinMode(enA, OUTPUT);
17      pinMode(enB, OUTPUT);
18      _in1 = in1;
19      _in2 = in2;
20      _in3 = in3;
21      _in4 = in4;
22      _enA = enA;
23      _enB = enB;
24    }
```

Figure 23.13 The constructor within the H-bridge library source file

```
34    void Hbridge::goForward()
35    {
36      digitalWrite(_in1, HIGH);
37      digitalWrite(_in2, LOW);
38      analogWrite(_enA, 255);
39      digitalWrite(_in3, HIGH);
40      digitalWrite(_in4, LOW);
41      analogWrite(_enB, 255);
42    }
```

Figure 23.14 Function definition within the H-bridge library source file

The weird double colon :: is called the *scope resolution operator*, and it used to define a function outside of its class. Don't worry if you don't understand this, but know that these are conventions that must be followed.

Finally, we have defined all of the other functions using the *scope resolution operator*, as done in Figure 23.14.

Notice that this looks almost identical to the function definition in our Dual_motor sketch with only a couple differences:

- After the word void we have included our library name (H-Bridge) along with the scope resolution operator (::). This tells the program that this function is part of the H-Bridge class.

- Each of our variables has an underscore in front of them: _in1, _in2, etc. This is a programming convention that helps humans remember which variables are private and which are public.

Completing and installing the library files

In order to use our H-Bridge library, we will first need to install these files into our Arduino libraries folder.

- Within your *Autonomous Robot Project* folder you will find a folder named *H-Bridge*. Open this folder, and then open the source file *Hbridge.cpp* with Notepad, TextEdit or another source code editor.
- The code in this file is incomplete in the same way that it was for the *Dual_motor* sketch (refer back to Table 23.1).
- Complete this code and save it.
- Add this *H-Bridge* folder to your Arduino's library collection by clicking on the Sketch menu and then selecting Include *Library* and then Add *.ZIP Library* (this folder does not need to be zipped). Refer to Figure 23.15.
- Find the *H-Bridge* folder and choose *Open*. This will install your new library ready for use.

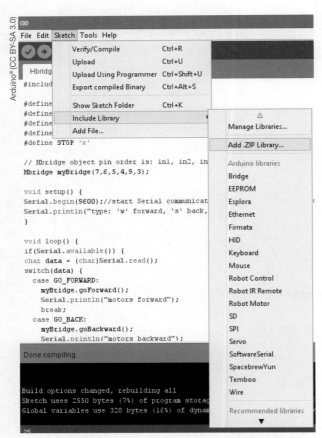

Figure 23.15 Installing a library into the Arduino IDE (the folder does not need to be zipped)

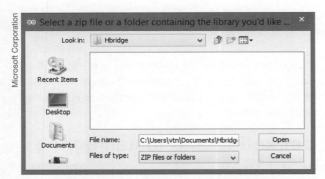

Figure 23.16 Click 'Open' when you have located the H-bridge folder

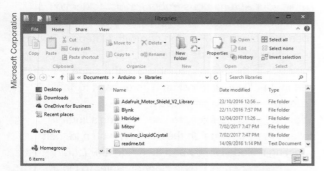

Figure 23.17 A folder containing your new library will automatically be created in the Arduino libraries folder when you include your library via the Arduino IDE

Creating an object to our H-bridge class

To use our H-Bridge library within an Arduino sketch, we simply need to include the library at the top of our code:

```
#include <Hbridge.h>
```

We can then create new *objects* using the standard naming convention by writing the name of the class 'H-Bridge' followed by a *space*, and then a *name* (of your choosing) followed by a set of parenthesis containing each of the required *arguments* (in this case the pin numbers for in1, in2, in3, in4, enA, and enB).

In our sketch we have created an object like this:

```
Hbridge myMotors1(7,6,5,4,9,3);
```

After you have done this you can use any of the functions and variables within the Hbridge class library by calling your object name with a full stop and the function name after it, like this:

```
myMotors1.goForward();
myMotors1.goLeft();
myMotors1.goRight();
```

From your *Autonomous Robot Project* folder, open the *Hbridge_class* sketch in to your Arduino IDE.

Run this code and test its functions using the same circuit set up that you used for the *Dual_motor* sketch (Figure 23.10).

If you wanted to use a second L298N module in your sketch to create a four-wheel drive vehicle then you could create a second object like this:

```
Hbridge myMotors2(13,12,2,8,11,10)
```

This should help you to understand that a class is like a blueprint that can be used to create other objects; kind of like cloning or creating an object from a mold.

PROJECT 5

Building and testing our robot

We have now created all of the code required to run our autonomous robot, and we should now have a good understanding of the systems, sub-systems and circuits.

In this project we are going to put our object sensing and motor movement systems together, and we are going to write an algorithm that will help our robot to avoid hitting objects.

Materials

- all of the resources that you used in Project 3
- an ultrasonic range finder (either 3 pin or 4 pin) with plastic holder
- a robot chassis kit with two DC motors and a pivot wheel
- an SPST switch (to turn your robot on and off)
- some extra breadboard jumper wires.

Figure 23.18 Robot chassis and motor kit

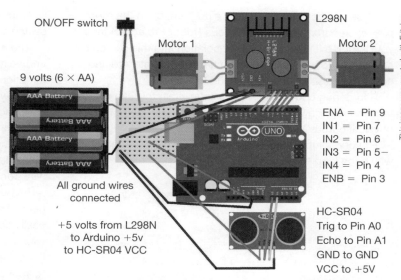

ON/OFF switch

L298N

Motor 1

Motor 2

9 volts (6 × AA)

AAA Battery
AAA Battery
AAA Battery
AAA Battery

ENA = Pin 9
IN1 = Pin 7
IN2 = Pin 6
IN3 = Pin 5−
IN4 = Pin 4
ENB = Pin 3

All ground wires
connected

+5 volts from L298N
to Arduino +5v
to HC-SR04 VCC

HC-SR04
Trig to Pin A0
Echo to Pin A1
GND to GND
VCC to +5V

This image was created with Fritzing.

Figure 23.19 Circuit setup for the autonomous robot. Note that the Arduino board is powered via the +5V out from the L298N module.

Figure 23.20 Underside of the robot chassis

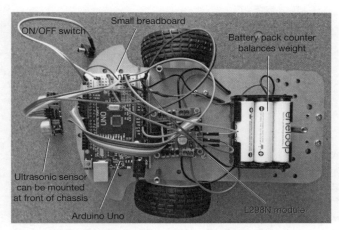

ON/OFF switch

Small breadboard

Battery pack counter
balances weight

Ultrasonic sensor
can be mounted
at front of chassis

Arduino Uno

L298N module

Figure 23.21 Component layout on the robot chassis

Assembling the robot

Assemble the robot chassis as per the instructions that came with your kit and by looking at the photographs above.

The battery pack should be placed over the swivel wheel to provide a counter balance. The Arduino, breadboard, and L298N module should fit neatly over the main wheels, leaving room for the ultrasonic sensor to be fitted at the front of the chassis (Figure 23.21).

Designing the algorithm

You will need to think about what you want your robot to do when it starts, and then what you want it to do when it encounters an object.

Use structured English to design your algorithm so that you can then convert this into Arduino code.

Your robot should take approximately 200 milliseconds to perform a quarter turn and one full second (1000 ms) for a 360° turn.

You should decide on the object sensing distance that will trigger a reaction from your robot, as well as how it will react.

Will it move backward, or move left or right? Will there be a combination of movements?

Use the commands: `myMotors.allOff()`, `myMotors.goForward()`, `myMotors.goBackward()`, `myMotors.goRight()`, `myMotors.goLeft();` and the `delay()` function to create your algorithm.

You can use the base of the structured English code that we used in Project 2 to prepare your algorithm.

```
robot_ping
WHILE
  Read echoPin
  Covert echoPin data to cm
    IF (//place your code here)
      // place your code here
    ELSE
      //Place your code here
    ENDIF
ENDWHILE
EXIT
```

Once you have finalised your algorithm, open the *robot_ping* sketch from your *Autonomous Robot Project* folder into your Arduino IDE and copy your solution into this sketch by converting your structured English algorithm into Arduino code (refer also to the algorithm in Project 2).

Add debug code at specific points within this sketch so that you can view code outputs and compare them with physical outputs if there is a problem.

Fit your solution into the structure that has been provided within the loop section of the *robot_ping* sketch:

```
void loop() {
int cm; // variable to hold the
   calculated distance of object

//cm = Ping3Pin(trigPin);// comment
   out this line if using a 4 pin
   sensor
cm = Ping4Pin(trigPin, echoPin);//
   comment out this line if using a 3
   pin sensor

if ( //place your code here ){
   // Place your code here
}
else {
// Place your code here
}
}
```

A complete solution for this sketch has been included in your *Autonomous Robot Project* folder in case you get stuck.

Making sure that the battery power on your robot is **switched off**, connect the Arduino on your robot to your computer with the USB cable and upload the *robot_ping* sketch.

Unplug the USB cable from your Arduino board and switch on the battery power to your robot.

The wheels of your robot should start moving almost immediately, and you should notice that they change direction when you place your hand in front of the sensor.

Test your robot by placing it on a hard surface next to a wall, and make note of the turning timings, and how your robot functions so you can make adjustments.

If your robot's motors appear to be moving in the opposite direction from what is expected, simply reverse the wire connections between the motor and L298N module.

If your robot did not work as expected then don't lose heart. This is a very complex system where things can easily go wrong. Go back over all of the steps, check your wiring, and upload the sample code (*robot_ping_complete*) if required. Turn the battery power off, connect your Arduino to your computer, and view the debug data in the serial monitor to see if you can troubleshoot the issue.

Please note: Depleted batteries will cause this system to malfunction, so make sure that you use fully charged batteries.

Upon successful completion of your robot, reflect on your team's performance and evaluate your completed prototype robot. You should discuss the following:
- the project's biggest challenges
- how your team overcame issues
- areas for improvement
- key skills and knowledge
- how well your team communicated.

9780170411820

THE TASK

This project is a more advanced version of line follower robot project from *Digital Technologies 7 & 8*. In that project you programmed a single sensor proportional line following robot.

In this project you will build the most advanced single sensor line follower program possible using a robot control method called PID. You may choose to work in a group or individually to design, program, code, test and evaluate your robot.

PID is how the cruise control on motor vehicles works.

Knowledge probe: PID explained

Knowledge Probe

The letters PID stand for proportional, integral, derivative.

Let's understand how the PID control system works first.

Proportional control measures the present

Say you wanted to reach a destination in a certain time and know that to do so you must maintain your car's speed at 60 kph.

The force with which you press the accelerator pedal and the speed of the car will be directly proportional. To maintain 60 kph, you will press harder when the speedometer drops below 60 kph and ease off when it rises above 60 kph.

This is like the robot proportional line follower program we built in *Digital Technologies 7 & 8*. The light measurement from the sensor was directly proportional to how close the sensor was to the edge of the line. The difference between the target light level and the sensor level was connected directly to steering. Proportional control measures the present!

Derivative control predicts the future

Say our car now begins to climb a steep hill. We need to press the accelerator rapidly to compensate for the sudden drop in speed to bring it back up to 60 kph. We are not just moving it proportionally any longer, but applying an instant fix for the sudden drop.

In a robot line follower program this would be like adding a new feature where steering can be turned extra sharply if a sudden change in light level is sensed (such as when the robot follows lines with tight turns). Derivative control predicts what will happen in the immediate future!

Integral control records the past

Using the above two controls we are now controlling both pedal distance to match a desired speed, and pedal adjustment to instantly fix the need for sudden acceleration or deceleration.

Imagine we have a target speed of 60 kph for our journey but have been driving at 59.8 kph and didn't notice the error. Over time, we would lose distance as the error would be too small to be adjusted by proportional control and since we are travelling steadily, it will not be picked up by derivative control.

Integral control adds these small errors over time and feeds them back as an adjustment to accelerator pedal distance. In the case of our robot, they are fed back to the steering control. Integral control collects what has happened in the past!

Total correction = **P** + **I** + **D**

= Proportional *adjusts for existing error*

+ Integral *adjusts by summing errors over time*

+ Derivative *adjusts for rate of change of error*

= current error × constant

+ total of all errors × constant

+ difference between last errors × constant

Note that these constants will not be all the same.

Defining

1 You will create three separate parts for your program in three stages: proportional (P), integral (I) and derivative (D).
   In the following we will assume the robot is following the left edge of the line. First we need to define the variables we will use. We will use Lego Mindstorms in the following explanation.
   Initialising variables to their correct starting values is important to make sure that when a program commences, left over values are not still being used. These are outlined in Table 24.1.

Acknowledgment for Figures 24.2–9 (on pages 154–7): LEGO® is a trademark of the LEGO Group of companies, which does not sponsor, authorise or endorse this publication.

Table 24.1

Variables needed	Set initial value to	Explanation
Target	Your desired colour sensor threshold (usually halfway between pure black and pure white); We will use 34%	The ideal light level from the colour sensor means it is exactly on line edge
Error	0	The difference between Target and what the sensor is now reading
Last error	0	The error the sensor read when it last went around our program loop
Integral	0	The sum of all errors so far (ideally zero)
Derivative	0	The difference between the last two errors

Designing

Building your robot

We recommend using the one sensor, two-wheel robot design from Chapter 26 of *Digital Technologies 7 & 8*.

It should have the following features:

- one colour sensor positioned approx. 10 mm from the surface
- two drive wheels
- a pivot point at the rear end.

Stage 1: Designing the proportional control

1 First position a loop for your program. This is going to grow quite long! It is possible to drag sections underneath others and reposition the lines showing the joins.

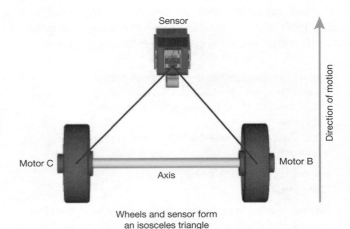

Figure 24.1 Viewed from above the robot, the sensor and wheels form an isosceles triangle.

Figure 24.2 Initialising variables

2 Define variables as listed in Table 24.1 using *variable blocks*, set each drop-down tab to *Write – numeric* and place them outside the loop as shown in Figure 24.2.

3 We created a proportional control in the project in Chapter 26 of *Digital Technologies 7 & 8*. This one is only slightly different because we need to capture the error value for reuse. We use:

error = target – sensor reading

Figure 24.3 shows how this is done.

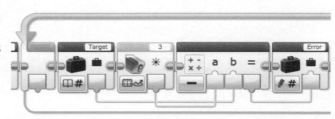

Figure 24.3 Finding the difference between target and sensor value

9780170411820

4 We read back this error value and multiply it by a constant to arrive at the proportional error. Here we will use b = 3 (as shown in the last red block in Figures 24.4 and 24.5) for our proportional constant.

Thus, our proportional control's adjustment value will be

P = error × some constant

Join these together to get the complete proportional calculation seen in Figure 24.5.

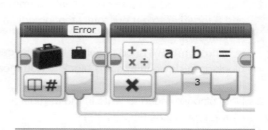

Figure 24.4 Multiplying the error by a constant (here 3)

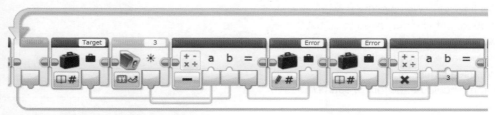

Figure 24.5 Final proportional control

Stage 2: Designing the integral control

We need to calculate:

integral = integral + error

and multiply this by a constant value (which we will need to adjust later).

Thus, our integral control's adjustment becomes:

I = integral × constant

In Figure 24.6, we show this 'b' constant set at 1 (see final red block in Figure 24.6), but if we set it to 0 we can deactivate the integral control for testing. Assemble code blocks as shown in Figure 24.6 and add it to your program code.

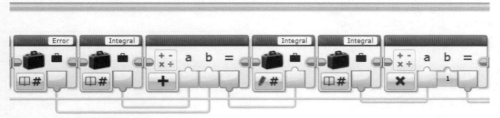

Figure 24.6 Final integral control

Stage 3: Designing the derivative control

1 We calculate:

derivative = error − last error (stored)

then multiply this by a constant value (which we will need to adjust later).

Thus, our derivative control's adjustment becomes:

D = derivative × constant

In Figure 24.7, we show this 'b' constant set at 1 (see final red block in Figure 24.7) but if we set it to 0 we can deactivate this derivative control for testing.

2 Construct the derivative control as shown in Figure 24.7.

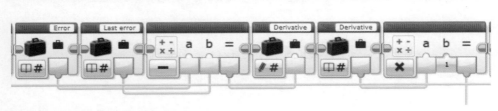

Figure 24.7 Final derivative control

Putting it all together

1   We need to add all three control values from Stages 1, 2 and 3 together to get our total steering adjustment value:
    Steering = P + I + D
    In Mindstorms we need to select the advanced maths block drop-down in a maths block to add more than two items.

2   Note also you need to write in the formula a + b + c in its top space (see Figure 24.8).

3   Connect the three outputs: P, I and D to the values a, b and c in this block to add them (see Figure 24.9).

4   Feed this result to a steering block as shown in Figure 24.8. Set it to 'On'. We have the power value as 26 in the illustration, but you may need to adjust this.

5   Finally, add two variable blocks to reset the last error variable to its new value, ready for the next journey through the loop (see Figure 24.8).

6   Your final program should be the join of each of these component parts:
    Figure 24.2 (initialising) + Figure 24.5 (proportional) + Figure 24.6 (integral) + Figure 24.7 (derivative) + Figure 24.8 (Final addition)
    Figure 24.9 shows the final version.

Implementing

1   Tuning your PID program will take patience! Turn off I and D controllers by setting the b values to 0 in the maths calculation blocks where they appear. (We already showed them as 0 in the above and Figure 24.9 has labels to show you where they are located.)

2   Experiment to find a suitable value for your proportional constant. (We have this set as 3 in Figure 24.9.)

3   Next, experiment with the value for the 'b' derivative constant until you are satisfied. Since this has to make big adjustments quickly, try 100 first.

4   Finally, fine-tune your PID by setting your 'b' integral constant. Try 0.01 first.

Evaluating

1   What did you learn by completing this project?

_____

_____

_____

_____

_____

_____

_____

_____

_____

_____

2   What would you do differently next time?

_____

_____

_____

_____

_____

_____

_____

_____

_____

_____

_____

_____

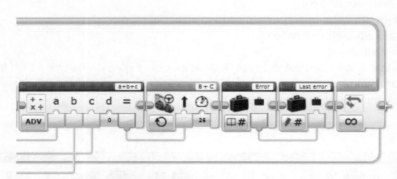

Figure 24.8 Final calculation with reset of last error

9780170411820

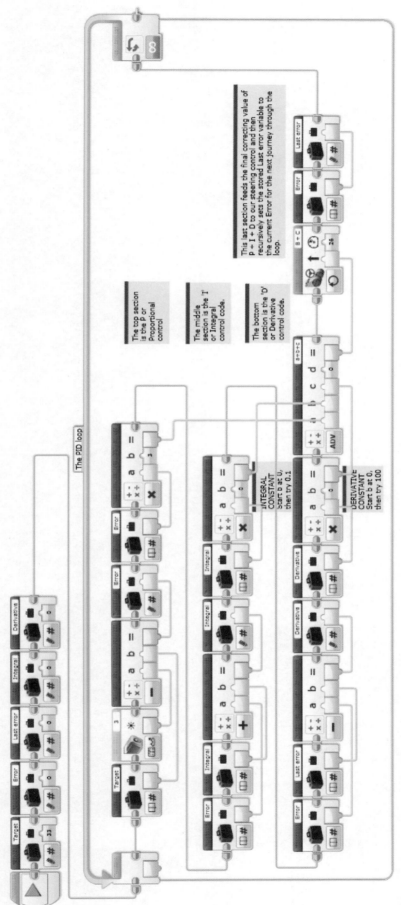

The PID loop

The top section is the P or Proportional control.

The middle section is the 'I' or Integral control code.

The bottom section is the 'D' or Derivative control code.

This last section feeds the final correcting value of P + I + D to our steering control and then recursively sets the stored Last error variable to the current Error for the next journey through the loop.

INTEGRAL CONSTANT Start b at 0, then try 0.1

DERIVATIVE CONSTANT Start b at 0, then try 100

Figure 24.9 The completed PID line follower code